795

D1527424

Match-Winning Tennis

By the same author

TENNIS: HOW TO BECOME A CHAMPION
YOUR BOOK OF TENNIS

Match-Winning Tennis

Tactics, Temperament and Training

C. M. JONES

FABER & FABER
3 Queen Square, London

First published in 1971
by Faber and Faber Limited
3 Queen Square, London W.C.1
Printed in Great Britain by
Western Printing Services Limited, Bristol
All rights reserved

ISBN 0 571 09289 6

Contents

73019

7

Introduction

Back in the year 1904 Admiral Hieachiro Togo achieved the ultimate in tactical perfection, thus annihilating the Russian fleet and hastening his country's final victory in the Japanese–Russian war.

Togo's tactical excellence owed much to his studies in England from 1871–8, when his principal tutor was Admiral Pakenham. As an observer from a neutral country Admiral Pakenham was barred by the rules of war from viewing his pupil's triumph from the bridge; his 'courtside' seat was on the deck below. From there he saw Togo so manoeuvre the Japanese fleet that he was able to 'cross the T': a perfection never before or since achieved in major naval warfare. By so doing Togo brought to bear on the stricken Russians every available gun in every single ship, while the Russians were able to reply only with the front guns of the leading ship of their line, which formed the upright of the 'T'.

While no man could ever in his wildest dreams expect to emulate either that pupil's or that teacher's achievement, it is my earnest hope that through this book I may serve as a lesser 'Pakenham' to thousands of little 'Togos' becoming ever more tactically adept in somewhat more joyful arenas: the tennis courts of Britain and the world.

1 · Spotting your Opponent's Weakness and Overcoming your Own

On June 26th, 1922, Lawn Tennis–which from then on came to be called colloquially 'tennis'–took a decisive step. Previously an exacting game favoured mainly by the financially comfortable, it suddenly moved into the realms of spectacle.

For that was the day on which the All England Lawn Tennis and Croquet Club moved its unique Wimbledon Championships from the old, essentially club ground at Worple Road to the spectator-orientated, new tennis complex at Church Road where the late King George V ensured the patronage of 'society' by performing the opening ceremony. More than that, he and his beloved Queen Mary became ardent fans, so encouraging tens of thousands to follow the fortunes of the stars of those days, primarily William Tatem ('Big Bill') Tilden, Gerald Patterson and Suzanne Lenglen.

It was an era of the individualist, a time when 'star quality' gushed from the giants in many fields, tennis among them, and in which personal satisfactions appeared less tied to the pursuit of money than in the Western World of the 1970s.

But spectacle attracts publicity and this, in its turn, nurtures ambition among performers. From the promoters' viewpoint, spectacle means cash-paying spectators, possible profits and the means of paying the never ending bills which pour in on every club treasurer.

By 1921 it was commonplace to tempt tennis stars to tournaments with offers of hospitality, transport, high life and, in some cases, cash under the table, an unforgivable sin in those days of Simon Pure amateurism. So 'shamateurism' grew from its embryonic state into a thriving infant before inexorably evolving into the highly complex state of affairs when it was possible to gather £10,000 sterling per annum as 'expenses' in the unreal, twilight tennis world prior to the arrival of 'Open' tennis in April 1968.

Spotting your Opponent's Weakness

Open tennis made possible championships in which each category of tennis player could compete against every other, so replacing the 'apartheid' of amateurs and professionals which had existed until then.

The first year, 1968, was quiet but 1969 erupted. Rodney Laver won in excess of $120,000 in prize money and drew an estimated $80,000 for endorsements and other side benefits. Stars like Tony Roche and John Newcombe edged past the $100,000, all in. Even these sums were topped by receipts in 1970 when managers of the calibre of Mark McCormack took over the business arrangements of the great public stars.

With so much at stake, success was no longer for the dilettante, not that it was in the 1930s, 40s or 50s. From the end of World War II, every minute detail of match winning became ever more important, and the combined genius and application of Jack Kramer, Pancho Gonzales and Rod Laver and the sheer industry of talented men like John Newcombe and Tony Roche blossomed into rich financial assets. Not that enjoyment ever left their souls. On their days off, after a lie-in and a round of golf, all were—and still are—to be found around the tennis matches.

So in advocating more intensive use of the brain and will when playing competitive tennis at any level, I am not offering hard graft in place of sheer pleasure. Indeed, the reverse is the case, except for the slothful. And I am yet to be convinced that the latter derive anything like the same satisfaction from life as those who stretch themselves to their limits in seeking to master challenges. To be totally involved is the meat and drink of life, and the pages which follow aim at increasing involvement in that great and subtle game, tennis, by way of its perhaps most fascinating aspect, strategy and tactics.

This aspect cannot be treated in isolation for it is inexorably related to physical and mental condition, to temperament and to techniques. The technical aspect of tennis has already been covered by my books *Tennis—How to become a Champion* and *Your Book of Tennis*. It is hoped that this book, by giving closer attention to tactics, temperament and training, will further enhance the reader's success and enjoyment in the game.

Firstly, to differentiate between strategy and tactics. The Oxford Dictionary definition of the former equates it to generalship: the management of an army in a campaign so as to impose on the enemy the place, time and conditions preferred for oneself. Tactics is described as the art of disposing one's army in actual contact with the enemy: the procedure calculated to gain some end.

When relating these terms to tennis, one's strokes, temperament, physical condition and intelligence together constitute the 'army' and the opponent represents the 'enemy'.

Careful study frequently suggests the objects one should have in mind when meeting an opponent. The tactics are the methods one adopts to bring about the achievement of those objects.

For example, having observed that a player's backhand was weak, one could go on court with three different objects: to break the stroke down completely, to direct shots to it in order to force weak returns that could easily be placed beyond his reach with the ensuing shot, or to leave that weakness alone for fear of the weak stroke becoming stronger, attacking it only when needing key points spaced along the course of the match. Jean Borotra employed this last method while beating René Lacoste in the 1924 Wimbledon singles final.

Manuel Santana provided another example when, in 1961, he beat Nicola Pietrangeli in the final of the French Championship to become the first Spaniard ever to win one of the world's four major singles titles.

Pietrangeli prefers hitting the ball on the run to making his strokes off returns coming to him. He is also a somewhat nervous player. So the strategy clearly was to hit the ball to him and, less clearly, to prey as much as possible on his nervousness.

In a nervous state of mind it is easier to deal instinctively with fast shots that do *not* allow too much time for anxious thought and to be presented with targets rather than to be forced to make one's own pace and targets. Santana capitalised on this by keeping the pace of his shots down and by withdrawing the target of passing shots by staying away from the net. Thus the theoretical strategy which evolved from study of this opponent achieved winning tactics and a rich reward.

There are often two or more ways of tackling the same player. The mighty Pancho Gonzales provides an example. Following his 312 minutes, 112 games record-breaking win over Charles Pasarell in the first round of the 1969 Wimbledon, Gonzales battled on to the fourth round where he met his great admirer and pupil Arthur Ashe.

Ashe reasoned that Gonzales, aged forty-one, would be somewhat tired from his efforts and, being tired, would react less quickly than normally. Consequently, Ashe sacrificed placement for speed, hitting every return as hard as possible, foreseeing quite correctly that Gonzales would not be able to move sufficiently quickly to counter effectively.

On the other hand, Tony Roche, who has beaten Gonzales on a number of occasions, uses diametrically opposite tactics which also take Gonzales's age into account. He sacrifices speed for acutely angled, low medium placed returns which force Gonzales to stretch, bend and make his own pace. Gonzales admits that Roche is the most tiring of all the opponents he meets. So there are two ways of playing the same man, each of them based on the conditions of the moment and, no less important, on the relative capabilities and temperaments of the tacticians.

However, if 'A' has weaknesses and tendencies, so has 'B'; consequently it is possible for each player to devise tactics calculated to baffle and beat the other. Theoretically, yes, but in practice, seldom. Strangely enough, only a handful of tennis players think as deeply as that about the game. Those who do think deeply generally hold high positions, so it is worth becoming a tactical and strategical expert. It is also great fun, mentally satisfying and financially beneficial.

The strategies and tactics adopted must be related to one's own capabilities and temperament. Clearly, a lightly built fellow of 5 ft. 6 in. is unlikely to possess the power of a mesomorphic athlete of 6 ft. 3 in. but he will almost certainly be more nimble. The taller man will be 95 per cent forced to adopt a 'power tennis' attitude towards his matches. The smaller will undoubtedly capitalise on nimbleness but he will have more choice. It is worth recalling that Jack Kramer, unquestionably one of the six greatest players in history, avers that Bobby Riggs provided the prototype for the modern 'big' game–and Riggs was small. So, too, were Henri Cochet and William Johnston. Cochet's net play was unbelievably effective and probably no man has ever stroked the ball with more ferocious power than Johnston.

Physical differences are obvious while temperamental ones generally lie hidden far below the surface. Indeed, they are so far down that possibly not one man or woman (from now on I shall use 'man' to include both sexes), in a thousand knows his own character other than superficially.

Temperamentally I suppose humanity divides into three main types: the adventurous, the phlegmatic and the anxious. Adventurous types are unlikely to succeed very often with 'safety first' methods. Those with a large anxiety quotient, however, can through intensive effort develop sufficient 'adventure' to become successful at taking risks. Initiative and adventure breed initiative and adventure–these tend to be self-generating and self-perpetuating qualities. Certainly they are capable of expansion.

On the other hand, a defensive attitude is ultimately demeaning and diminishing. So to succeed as a defensive player calls for enormous self-discipline.

The test comes only in a crisis, especially in a crisis against an opponent reputedly inferior but nevertheless close enough to offer real danger of defeat. Ask yourself, 'How do I react in such situations?' and answer honestly.

There is in the animal kingdom a seemingly inherent 'pecking order'. Hens will line up in a very definite order to peck, one going naturally to the head of the queue, another to second place and so on down to the end. Be assured that this applies in the human world, especially in tennis. Most of us know or have seen men and women who automatically go to the front in any situation as if by divine right. They are the people who always get the only taxi or are served first in a restaurant or receive the best attention in a shop. No less on a tennis court, there are some who appear to triumph because it is their right: they establish and maintain an ascendancy in the 'pecking order' that always seems to hold good in the end, no matter how far behind they may lag at first.

Sven Davidsson, the only Swede to have won one of the world's top four (Wimbledon, the French, Australian and U.S.A. Championships) singles titles, was an outstanding example. He claimed with complete justification that he could always beat Nicola Pietrangeli or Jacques Brichant—two major European rivals of his day—no matter how poor his form because he could always dominate them mentally. His results against them in big events justified his words.

However, though the relevance of the 'pecking order' to tennis is scarcely, if at all, understood, men are creatures of free will. There need be nothing immutable or eternal about one's own place in that order. Mere realisation of its existence is a first salvo towards becoming its master. Any person can raise himself in it. Helen Wills, at worst the third best woman player in history, used to lull herself to sleep each night by constant repetition of the words 'I can and I will'.

She did, to the tune of winning the women's singles at Wimbledon the record number of eight times. Undoubtedly she rated high in the 'pecking order' by nature, but she took great pains to ensure she moved higher up it. This implies, correctly, that every thought, every action, every moment spent in training and practice must be pregnant with purpose and determination. As Lilian Board once said so truly on B.B.C. radio, 'gold medals are won in training'.

No ball—not one—should be struck in practice with any thought other than 'I intend to be a better player after this shot than I was before it'. This is not easy to achieve. In competition there are the twin stimuli of an opponent to beat and a prize to win. It is so easy to be purposeful and determined. There he is, only 26 yards away. The final or semi-final is only a match or two ahead. Probably other competitors are milling around or chatting with officials and others in positions to help them and you. It is all too easy.

In training you are usually on your own. This is where self-discipline comes in. Now is the time when an embryonic champion shows up. Not a moment is wasted. Every tactical move is played out on the court. Time is as valuable as plutonium.

Spotting your Opponent's Weakness

If it is a session of physical training the champion goes on until his body shrieks for a rest . . . and then runs another mile . . . and then undertakes some further exercises. Time and again he forces himself through and beyond the immediate pain until such pain becomes almost unreal. His body may suffer it but his brain is detached: calmly assessing what must or must not be done to seize more points and games; to overcome the opponent and win the match.

It is worth noting here that natural introverts are somewhat better at breaking through the pain barriers of training and practice than extroverts. However, do not despair. Long term, scientific personality researches have proved beyond question that application improves anyone's ability to withstand mental pressures and physical pain; the extroverts do indeed move along the continuum towards introversion.

Consequently, always extemporise to make training tougher than match play. Emulate squash star Jonah Barrington who, to give but one positive example of his attitude, once realised that any man who could, in one rally, force him to play 50 consecutive high backhands would probably win the point; to counter this possible tactical weakness he used to go on court alone and hit runs of 200 high backhands; to practise situations four times harder than the very hardest he would ever meet in match play. His reward came in the final of the 1969 British Open Championship when, after five recent losses to world champion Geoff Hunt, he devised tactics which put the highest possible premium on his own stamina and mental toughness while countering the superior power and variety of Hunt.

In working out training-practice schedules be utterly ruthless in winkling out your weaknesses and cruelly calculating in devising systems for rectification.

Development of speed provides a case, for there can be few men other than Rod Laver who would not be better if they could only increase their speed. Not their speed over a 100 yards dash but in making that first move at the net or in taking those first two steps when hastening to a wide or short return.

Speed of this nature largely depends on your power-weight ratio—in effect, on your brute strength. Reaction time, eyesight and other factors enter into it, but muscle explosiveness is mainly

17

a product of brute strength. Develop strength without adding proportionate weight and bulk and your speed must be increased.

Bear in mind, though, the relative difficulty of transference. Practise 100 yard sprints and there will be some improvement on the tennis court. But the main benefit will come in your reduced time for a 100 yards sprint. Better, therefore, to practise short dashes on a tennis court towards imaginary balls hit by an opponent. Do the job thoroughly by having a racket and making imaginary shots.

Better still, do a couple of potato races and then go straight on court with *two* practice opponents, posting them at the net with a bucket of tennis balls.

Let them fire one ball at you and then volley your returns here, there and everywhere for you to chase at your very fastest speed. The moment you miss they fire another – and another and another. Five minutes of this 'threesomes' practice will have you gasping for breath but if you undertake such practices every day, over a period of months your speed off the mark and about the court will bound forward.

There is an important rider. It is vital each time to drive yourself right through all barriers and beyond your seeming limits of speed and endurance. You must be utterly determined to increase your speed.

All this is relatively easy when things are going well. The champion perseveres relentlessly throughout a spell of disappointments. Indeed, he does more. He intensifies his efforts, perhaps in quantity, certainly in quality.

There is another important point to be made and that is the need for a long term view. Training for today's big match should have begun twelve months ago, even if the specific tactics were devised yesterday. For if those tactics are simply net attacks following a 'short to the forehand long to the backhand' sequence of shots, such a sequence should have become automatically grooved through daily practice for at least a year – as should many other sequences.

Such sequences – like all practices which demand intensive mental as distinct from physical effort – should be perfected in short spells of eight, nine or ten minutes at a time. They can be undertaken one after the other, so that developing an armoury of ten basic sequences will occupy the best part of one and three-quarter hours a day.

The reason for this is explained fully in my book *Tennis, How to Become a Champion*,[1] but, briefly, thinking of a movement electrically 'grooves' the muscles to make that movement more and more efficiently but after a while—five minutes, perhaps, for an extrovert, ten for an introvert—the mind goes into a state of 'waking sleep' in which true mental control is lost. Thus one is likelier to practise and, consequently, 'groove' the wrong thing than the right. Rest prevents this and, as the old saying so truly points out, 'a change is as good as a rest'.

Motivation plays an important part. Performance is a product of habit (achieved through intelligent practice) and drive. Drive derives from many factors, among which motivation rates highly. If the motivation is intense (swim or die) the length of time one can effectively continue one set of operations is considerably longer than when the motivation is low.

Today one frequently hears the expression 'playing the percentages'. This means using the tactics or playing the shot which gives you the greatest chance of success with the smallest risk of failure. It often involves a split-second choice between playing the 'right' shot which, unfortunately, is not one of your best, or the 'wrong' shot, which happens to be your particular *forte*.

Jack Kramer put it specifically[2]:

'Every tournament competitor should learn what is meant by "playing the percentages".

'Essentially, this means using the shots you know you can make at the crucial time. It does not help at all to know that the right shot is a top spin, fast, cross-court forehand hit hard because your opponent is camped on the net if you can only keep that shot in court once out of twenty times.

'Instead, you have to take your chance with the shot you can play—maybe a forehand down the line—and hope that the man at the net won't volley the ball beyond your reach.

[1] Faber and Faber.
[2] *Lawn Tennis* (the official journal of the L.T.A.) January 1970, page 13.

'To give another example, you cannot expect to put the ball away from a deep position, so why try? You cannot put away an approach shot inside the service court if the ball is below net height, so why try? Instead, minimise your chances of erring on those shots.

'When returning a strong service, you know you can only make so many passing shots. So unless you are playing a super volleyer, why try? Let him play a volley, preferably off a return near his ankles. Maybe you will have a better chance of passing him next shot or perhaps he may even miss his volley.

'Learn to think for yourself from this moment so that you are always playing the ball or positioning yourself in such ways that you increase your own chances of winning points and decreasing your opponents.'

There are two caveats which must be written. Firstly, 'playing the percentages' slowly develops a calculating mind but there are moments in big tennis when calculation must be subservient to courage and adventure. Moments when one must throw all previous knowledge away and stake all on one blinding play or stroke. Such gambles demand complete freedom from inhibition. 'I can and I will' is the order of the day, for there is surely no truer saying than 'Fortune favours the brave' or, if you prefer, 'you make your own luck'. Never was this better demonstrated than when Ted Schroeder beat Frank Sedgman in the 1949 Wimbledon quarter finals. Down match point, Schroeder served, rushed for the net and was dragged back to the service line by the cruel call 'foot fault'. Unhesitatingly and unflinchingly, he served strongly and again rushed in, this time to win the point with his third volley. Altogether he saved three match points with brave play that simply defied Sedgman to beat him.

Yet if his spirit had been brave but his performance cautious, he would surely have lost. These were the moments when bravery rated far higher that playing the percentages. They occur fairly often. You must learn to recognise them when they do and develop the guts to stake all unreservedly.

Secondly, playing the percentages can make it easy for an astute opponent to read your intentions. This, indeed, is one of the fallacies of so-called 'killer instinct', as will be demonstrated in Chapter 8.

This rightly suggests that surprise is an important factor in good tactics. I vividly recall Juan Couder beating Neale Fraser in the Italian championships. For four hours and twenty minutes they struggled, with Couder serving his lollypops and remaining every time on the baseline. Eventually he reached match point and served the lollypop to end all lollypops, almost reaching the net before the ball in his headlong race forwards. Normally Fraser would have blasted such a sacrificial offering to perdition but, such was his sheer disbelief in Couder's net rush, he tamely mis-hit the ball into the bottom of the net.

Surprise also slows an opponent's reaction time. Habit (practice) makes one's muscles more efficient in performing special duties. They operate automatically; the movements become reflex. Surprise imposes changes, entails learning new replies, unlearning old ones. The mind works quickly but not infinitely quickly. If one gains a tenth of a second at the net that can represent an extra yard or more of coverage, more than the difference between a winning volley and a losing passing shot. That is a simple example. More complex ones will arise later.

There is one generality still which must be covered, namely 'never change a winning game'. That is only a half truth. Any player of similar calibre to yourself will raise his game or change his tactics as defeat draws ever nearer.

If he is not of similar standard, you are either going to win or lose almost irrespectively of the tactics you adopt; you will outclass or be outclassed and the gap can only be lessened over time on the practice court.

The better saying is: 'When playing an opponent of similar standard be ready to intensify a winning game'. You take the first set by attacking. Seek to hit harder and mistakes may well creep in. But, encouraged by success, try moving six inches or so nearer to the pitch of the ball for your shots and the effect will be similar with far less danger of mistakes.

One cannot legislate for the infinite number of situations that arise in tennis match play. The only valuable generalisations are to study tennis and to keep the mind free at all times from inflexibility. It is good to be so technically adept that you can outplay your opponent. It adds immeasurably to the pleasure and the profit when you can also out-think him.

There is one other point—an important one—which must be made. The use of good tactics is essential to success but they can never be absolute; there come points, games, perhaps even sets where the tactically correct play can be asking for trouble. The same sequence repeated *ad nauseum* loses all its surprise element and, therefore, much of its value.

Tactics are a tool which you have to use. You must be the judge of when and how best to use any particular ruse. The theories in this book are sound but they are not inviolate. The thought 'always do so and so' should not be applied to anything written here or in any other book. But by thought, study and competitive play your ability to discern when or when not to do this, that or the other should constantly develop, and with it your skills in using your technical attributes to the greatest advantage. In short, you should learn to win more matches than you do now.

2 · Finesse and Power in Men's Singles

There are several ways of beating your opponent in singles. You can serve so fast and accurately that he never returns the ball; then eventually you break his service to win each set.

You hit so hard and accurately that every shot evades him.

You can volley so decisively and cover the net so completely that he can never hit the ball beyond your reach.

Your control of spin and placement may be so superior that you can manoeuvre your opponent like a puppet on a string until he makes a mistake or leaves a wide gap into which a winning shot can safely be hit.

You can return the ball so consistently and with such variation of pace, length and spin that he falls into constant error.

You can mix these various systems, or some of them, so astutely that he does not know if he is coming or going.

The type of surface on which you play is an important factor. On the red hard courts seen so often in England and on the European continent—called 'clay courts' in many parts of the world—the bounce of the ball is high and slow so that defence is more efficacious than on closely clipped, dry turf where, the surface resistance being low so that the ball skids through, the bounce is low and fast. Wooden courts are even faster; so, too, are those of cement rubbed smooth by constant years of play. Artificial turf like Nygrass is not as fast as the natural grass at Wimbledon but is about the same speed as average, good, well cut but not closely cropped grass. On all these fast courts aggression is mostly more effective than defence among players of equal standard.

Here let 'aggression' be defined for tennis. It does not mean hitting every ground stroke, volley or service with every ounce of your strength. The unexpected drop shot when your opponent expects a deep drive, or a disguised low, fast lob over his head when he is poised at the net ready to cut off any passing shot, is just as aggressive as any powerful drive. Initiative is

23

more relevant to aggression than power, though in the final stages of a close match power tends to be a trustier ally than accuracy. Thus any would-be champion should seek to develop one crushing stroke in his armoury for judicious use at all times and special exploitation in crises.

Nevertheless, this does not negate the general rule of tennis that something like two out of every three points are won through mistakes, often silly mistakes. On this basis there are three special axioms that should always be borne in mind.

Arthur Roberts, one of the world's greatest coaches, always instils into his pupils: 'I'll get the ball back or bust.' The late Wilfred Austin drummed into his children, and into me, 'The main and primary object of the game of lawn tennis is to hit the ball over the net.' The third axiom is: 'Treat each ball on its merits.'

Neither of the first two results in a negative attitude, especially when together it is related to treating each ball on its merits. Indeed, this is one of the finest aids to concentration I know.

Consider the saying 'Tall oaks from little acorns grow'. Now ally this to the number of times you hear tournament players say to themselves, 'I must win this match' or 'I must win this set' or 'I must win this game, or this point'. I would be considerably richer if I had £1 for every time I heard one of those remarks.

Yet consider how points, games, sets and matches are won: by winning strokes, maybe a few; but mostly by making fewer mistakes, especially on key points, than the opponent. To avoid mistakes every possible scrap of concentration should be applied to the shot being played; to the direction of the oncoming ball, its pace, spin and trajectory; to the possible positions the opponent is taking up; to the geometrical patterns arising from his shot and the one you are about to make. Perhaps to the actual technique of your stroke, though techniques should largely be automatic by the time you are engaged regularly in competitive play.

How can the mind be fully occupied with such immediacies if you are thinking 'I must win this game'?

Sufficient unto the day . . . Treat each and every ball on its merits for that will keep you fully occupied during the early part of your plan to improve.

The early result of this policy may well be too many defensive returns which your opponent will place beyond your reach. This is where 'each ball on its merits' begins to work in your favour. If you are truly disciplined to this policy, your concentration on the shot in hand will very quickly get the message through to you. You are not doing enough with the ball. Too many of your returns are unnecessarily soft or poorly placed; you are not treating each ball on its merits. So discrimination based on good concentration will begin to work. Many returns will still be defensive but those shots of your opponent which merit harsher treatment will receive it. In discriminating you will begin to learn the regular sequences of shots which characterise tennis matches.

Now comes another key moment in tactical development. You will have to ask yourself: 'Are my placements governed by the ball and the way it comes to me or am I dictating to the ball?'

Top stars always govern the ball. For example, they seldom hit the ball down the line because that is what the oncoming ball suggests is natural or easy. They think what is best and do it.

From this platform you will begin to think sequentially and in hitting each ball will have some thought about the ensuing shots. In men's tennis on fast courts the sequences will be short; modern men's tennis abounds in serve-return-winning volley points. . . . Except when men like Laver, Roche, Newcombe and Drysdale are engaged. Each in his manner tries to manoeuvre his opponent around the court. All are expert in executing shrewdly angled returns which tease volleyers, open wide gaps and set up opportunities for winning strokes on the fourth, sixth, eighth or later shots in the rally.

A close study of them in championship action shows the immense discrimination they use in dealing with each ball sent over by their opponent. Probably their applied concentration has become so habitual that they scarcely realise it is happening. Yet it does happen.

Note the phrase 'applied concentration', for this is the ideal to which all who seek improvement should aspire. Most players feel they are concentrating well if they keep their minds within the confines of the court. The expert in applied concentration is so immersed in analysing his opponent's strengths, tendencies and weaknesses, devising tactics and methods to exploit them and generally scheming for victory that there is simply no chance for his mind to wander.

Laver provided an example of how a champion applies his mind when completing his 1962 'Grand Slam' of the Australian, French, Wimbledon and American singles championships.

Then far less dangerous on clay courts than on grass, he knew the French singles would offer the greatest danger to his ambition. His fears were amply justified when Martin Mulligan reached match point against him in the quarter finals. Laver was serving and he had the choice of going for an ace or . . . what? His mind alert, he served his first ball at three-quarter pace to Mulligan's backhand and ran fast for the net, covering the down-the-line shot. Mulligan duly returned the ball down the line and Laver volleyed the ball across the court yards beyond the reach of Mulligan's desperately groping racket.

He explained later that Mulligan has a marked preference for down-the-line backhands when he is not given time to think, and that if he, Laver, had tried for an ace and faulted, Mulligan would have had time with the slower second service to hit the ball either down the line or across the court. 'If he had gone across court I would have been helpless,' Laver confessed later.

Here was a masterly example not only of applied concentration but also of change of pace—or, to be precise, choice of the right pace for the situation.

Drobny showed equal sensitivity when winning the last point of his 1954 Wimbledon singles against Rosewall. As he walked back to serve he reasoned that Rosewall would be expecting and, therefore, keyed up to slam back an attempted ace. He would also adjust himself quickly to deal summarily with a very slow service. So Drobny sent over one which was neither so fast that the ball would come back via a Rosewall reflex stroke nor so slow that quick-thinking and quick-moving Rosewall could adjust his position and hit a winner. His three-quarter pace service carried just sufficient spin to add to the confusion. The effect was all that he could have hoped for: Rosewall returned the ball tamely into the net.

Contrast this with Rosewall's final against Newcombe in the

1967 BBC 2 tournament. Rosewall had six chances in four sets to break service, winning five of them and returning the ball on the sixth, although the service was ultra fast and looked an ace until the ball suddenly went back into court. Not strong enough to prevent Newcombe from scoring a winner but, still, Rosewall returned a seeming ace into play.

The essence of success in changes of pace, length and direction is subtlety. Any change devoid of subtlety must lack one of the essential ingredients – surprise.

Perhaps the best use of changed length in post-war Wimbledon came from the Australian left-hander Mervyn Rose in 1952 when he met the holder, Dick Savitt, on court one. Savitt was one of the greatest ground stroke players since the end of World War II.

Savitt had bludgeoned his way through the 1951 singles by tremendous hitting with both his forehand and backhand that overwhelmed his opponents. In the final the giant Australian Ken McGregor endeavoured to overcome him with a strong serve-volley attack based on orthodox methods. His long serves and deep approach drives merely fed fuel to a fire. Savitt rifled the ball down the lines or across the court beyond the reaching racket of 6 ft. 3 in. McGregor, who failed to win a set.

Rose realised the futility of attempting to repeat McGregor's methods and, instead, reversed them. Hitting his first shots deep, he sliced his subsequent shots in each rally short and closed in on the net. Forced to hurry forward, Savitt was prevented by the short length and low bounce from hitting the ball with his customary power. Simultaneously his relative closeness to the net reduced the angles open to his passing shots. Rose, a man of rapid reflexes and fast movements, was able to cut off the returns and volley his way to the major surprise win of the fortnight. It was a great triumph for a subtle campaign based on both changes of length and spin.

Changes of angle are, perhaps, more difficult to devise. One of the most useful arises during serving when it is possible and profitable to mix deliveries which swing away across the opponent's forehand with others which swing into his right elbow. Very few players are comfortable with such in-swingers. This discomfort is even more marked when the server is left-handed.

It was a significant factor in the ascendancy Rod Laver achieved over Ken Rosewall in the years 1968 and 1969. Rosewall is one of the greatest returners of service in tennis history. In-swingers to his forehand were his only slight vulnerability. It was very slight but in the highest classes of tennis minute margins decide the outcome of championships.

Important as the skills I have been describing may be, combined with accuracy, they tend to be less trustworthy in crises than sheer power. It is a physiological fact that danger galvanises the adrenal gland into action—colloquially the 'fight or flight' syndrome—and this normally sharpens the senses and speeds the reactions.

A personal experience provides a classic example. Driving from Dover to London I suddenly found my vision obliterated by a frosted windscreen which had been hit by a flying stone. It seemed to me an appreciable period elapsed while I recalled the advice I had read and then punched out the windscreen with my fist. My wife, in the passenger seat, said in surprise 'Why did you smash the windscreen?' It had all happened so quickly that she had not realised the windscreen had frosted first.

So it is in tennis. The drop shot which leaves the opponent flat footed in the opening games is spotted instantaneously and picked up at five–all in the final set.

The drive or volley hit within three inches of a line may be an outright winner at two–all. At five–four in the final set the increased adrenalin flow resulting from the danger will give a brave opponent an extra pace or more ease of movement and the drive will be returned. So the touch player must seek to drop the ball even closer to the net or aim his drive at the line instead of three inches inside it. The percentage chances of success decrease rapidly and swing over to the opponent.

Touch, accuracy, variety, subtlety must remain valuable weapons but it behoves the champion to have at his command the ultimate, decisive weapon, power.

It should be fully understood that this is a generalisation, that there are always exceptions. Yet study the list of Wimbledon men's singles champions from 1946 to 1969. In those twenty-four championships only Manuel Santana can be classed as a predominantly 'touch' player. All the rest, including that master tactician Jaroslav Drobny, exploited a power to finesse ratio ranging from 90:10 (McKinley, Emerson, Trabert?) to 60:40 (Drobny?).

Savitt's 1951 Wimbledon win demonstrated the need for another tactical skill—pacing a match wisely. It arose in the semi-final in which Herbert Flam stormed his way to a one set, five games to one lead. Such was the speed and intensity of Flam's buzzing attacks that Savitt himself had to laugh in semi-despair. Perhaps Flam was afraid to reduce the intensity a degree or two in case he let Savitt into the match. Certainly he continued to attack at a furious pace; Savitt geared his game up to it and once he started his climb back Flam possessed no deeper reserves on which to draw.

In contrast, Laver is normally reluctant to begin in top gear, fearing always that the let-down which almost inevitably follows will allow his opponent to establish an unbreakable hold on the match. On the other hand, there are occasions when it pays to start at top speed in order to work oneself up into a sufficiently confident mood to overcome a resourceful defender or to inhibit a determined aggressor. Occasionally I used this system when I was a prolific tournament winner; but these occasions were few compared with the times when the slow build-up seemed preferable.

On this basis I am always fearful of the man who 'throws' sets. Unless you rank among the world's top forty players, there will be matches you must almost surely lose and others it will be extremely difficult to lose.

The key matches, those which provide the stepping stones to improvement and advance, are those against opponents slightly your superior. In such matches you employ every scrap of your skill and effort, sometimes to establish an early lead of, perhaps, a couple of sets. Such ascendancies must be maintained with every ounce of determination you possess.

Probably the effort has been intense and you are momentarily drained. Your opponent breaks service early in the third set, and then again to lead 4–1. The temptation to relax and make another big effort in the fourth set can be overwhelming. It is possible that this is the correct move. The danger, an immense one, is twofold: your own inability to recapture your earlier spark and your opponent's confidence now that he has begun to climb out of a losing position.

Winning against opponents of similar standard to your own is predominantly a matter of will and concentration. Both must be harnessed completely to the achievement of victory. Throwing sets seriously jeopardises your maintenance of full will and concentration. The gambit can be effective but for every occasion I have seen it succeed I can recall several where it has failed.

If you consider you must throw a set, do so purposefully. Avoid the trap of deceiving yourself that you will practise some particular shot or will run your opponent around—possibly by alternating drop shots and lobs—because running unaccompanied by mental or psychological pressure imposes only minimal demands on a fit, eager man or woman. How many times have you seen a player develop cramp in practice or friendly play? Never; once; perhaps twice? I would gamble never more. Yet cramp is relatively commonplace in tournament tennis. Physical effort unaccompanied by mental pressure tires men only slowly. So if you must throw a set, be sure to maintain full concentration yourself and, somehow, impose such mental pressures as you can on your opponent.

One reads great tracts about the power of Pancho Gonzales, the amazing net coverage of Frank Sedgman, the non-stop, hustling aggression of Chuck McKinley, the brave way in which Rod Laver goes for breathtaking shots when the chips are down.

Seldom, however, is one reminded of another major facet of their greatness—scrambling ability. All these champions, and many more, are or were much feared by their opponents for their willingness to chase down the, apparently, most impossible shots, to hoist the ball back into play as best they can, and to chase yet again when the ball is blasted into another corner.

No champion I can recall was ever too proud to look foolish while being chased around the court by a lesser man. Indeed, such stupid thoughts seldom, if ever, occurred to them. There was the ball, somehow it had to be returned and the rally continued. And that is all there was to it.

No one ever wins a 'cheap' point in big matches against such men. Undoubtedly, scrambling ability is one of the hallmarks of champions. Like many assets, it increases with use, so start chasing everything today. Never let any ball go by without making a supreme effort to reach it. Immediately you will be surprised by how many 'impossibilities' you quickly achieve. In two months' time or so many balls that once evaded your racket by six feet will only be three feet away and a few months later still you will get your racket to them.

Certainly, speed of reflex and of foot are vital but I am convinced that even more important is that old-fashioned virtue, intestinal fortitude—in plain language, guts.

Your legs and arms may be aching, your head heavy, your breath coming in painful gasps. Don't give in. Force yourself to race at top speed after your opponent's fast cross-court drive. Never let go. When he slams your answering weak offering down the line, chase the ball again. Chase it with fierce mental determination and control so that when you reach the ball—and you will do so more often than you expect—you have the wit and will not to slash out wildly, in despair. Instead, you squeeze out one extra pace and while the ball is nearing its second bounce some reserve of thought enables you, perhaps, to dink the ball across the court or hoist a deep lob that catches him by surprise.

First, make it your habit to chase everything, but everything. Closely second, learn to detach your thinking so that you think through and over pain and mental anguish to play shrewd, calculated returns that give the minimum to the man across the net.

Never surrender. Never give him a 'cheap' point. Make him win every point that goes to him on the score sheet. No other attitude can take you to the top.

In your chasings do not become annoyed by your opponent's good shots. Accept that they are good, that he is skilful and then determine to be even more skilful. If the gap is too wide to bridge in one day, learn from his example and incorporate his shots or methods into your own game through assiduous practice. If he beats you again next time, chide yourself for not having learned your lesson well enough and redouble your efforts to advance.

Finesse and Power in Men's Singles

Gonzales has the right attitude. 'When someone makes a good shot I accept it,' he told me once, 'then I think to myself "and now I will show you a better one".' In that way he used other men's talents to improve his own.

Scrambling is important on any surface but especially so on clay courts. These, because of their composition, resist the flight of the ball and cause it to bounce significantly more slowly than on closely cut grass.

The faster the surface, the greater the premium on power and aggression. Men's play at Wimbledon becomes boring at times, so strongly is it monopolised by exponents of the 'serve–run to the net–volley system'. Yet South Africa's Cliff Drysdale and Spain's Manuel Santana have shown on grass courts that accurate and controlled ground strokes can earn positions ranging from first to fourth in the world whilst aggressors like Tony Trabert have won the French Championship which is virtually the world championship on clay.

Fast courts simplify attacking methods but attack is still vital on even the slowest surface. All too often attack is equated with speed. Anyone who has seen Drobny tear the heart and lungs out of a helpless 'world top-tenner' with mixtures of drop-shots, lobs and acutely angled ground strokes will confirm that attack comes clothed in many guises.

It is necessary to exercise more patience and discrimination in choosing the right ball to force when on clay. Yet when that ball comes it must be attacked with just as much, possibly even more, determination than the weak shot offered to you on grass courts. Attack is usually thought to be a matter of technique. That is but one quarter the truth. Attack—maybe initiative is a better term—derives from a positive attitude of mind which seeks always to make the most effective use of every ball coming across the net.

So, in general, treat each ball on its merits, chase everything, never surrender and be alert always for the chance to harry and surprise your opponent.

3 · Baseline Play

The fundamental aim of a baseline player is to overcome his opponents by quality of ground stroke play.

That quality may be represented by power, accuracy, consistency, variety, subtlety or, more likely, by mixtures of all these assets.

Dick Savitt won Wimbledon in 1951 primarily through the power and accuracy of his ground strokes. On the other hand, men like Josef Asboth, Fausto Gardini and 'Beppi' Merlo were formidable competitors because they mixed consistency, accuracy and subtlety with ground-stroke skill.

It is important to distinguish between consistency and accuracy. Consistency means hitting the ball back time and time again without error but with no special regard to length or placement. Accuracy means hitting the ball repeatedly within inches of the desired spot. Usually accuracy and consistency go hand in hand and there is strong correlation between the two terms where tennis is concerned. But while consistency implies freedom from error, an accurate player can also be dogged by a modicum of inconsistency. Specifically then, a man like Rosewall or a woman in the Ann Jones mould should be labelled 'accurate and consistent' in any serious analysis.

As in all tactical situations, the object of a baseliner should be to bring his strongest weapons to bear on his opponent's weakest, and never to permit him any chance of converting such weakness into a strength.

To do this effectively, it is vital to understand the percentage chances of hitting a ball beyond the reach of your opponent. Examine this plan of a court (Fig. 3A). If you are at A and your opponent at B the chances of hitting a winner against him are remote; four or five to one against, at best. So why try? Why skim the net with a fast drive aimed within an inch or so of one of the lines in his court? Unless he is far below your standard, he will reach and return the ball.

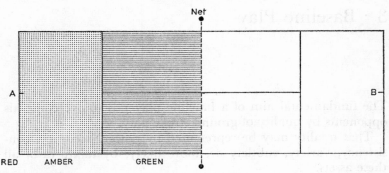

Figure 3A

Traffic light tennis. Your chances of hitting a winner from the red zone behind the baseline are slender, so why take the risk? Unless your opponent is at the net, hit the ball high enough over the net for it to bounce near the other baseline.

Shots played in the amber zone may merit aggression – proceed with care.

In the green area the odds should favour attack.

Better, then, to give the ball plenty of air over the net and to try a safely angled return that moves him towards or beyond one of the sidelines. Maybe his next return will be shorter so that you can hit it from somewhere in the part of the court shaded by diagonal lines. The odds are still slightly against your hitting a winning drive, how much against depends on the placement of your preceding shot.

However, from a more advanced position the height of the net relative to the length of the court is reduced. Then, too, your range of possible angles is increased from a more forward position. You should be able to put him in even greater difficulties with your second shot. Maybe, in such difficulties, his next return will pitch in the horizontally lined part of the court.

This is the area of the court from which you must press home your attack. Bear in mind the danger of hitting over the baseline if the ball is struck below the level of the net. Then top spin should be imparted in order to make the ball dip in its flight. Yet top spin or not, the chance and need to attack must overrule other considerations. If the ball bounces above net level you should be able to place the ball out of reach two-thirds of the time.

Baseline Play

If it is below net level a deep drive which you follow to the net may be preferable. Whatever you decide, the key note must be attack.

This system was first devised by American master coach Mercer Beasley who gave, among others, Ellsworth Vines and Frank Parker to tennis. He named it 'traffic light tennis': the area behind the baseline representing red, the diagonal stripe section amber and the horizontal stripe position green.

Every section and all advice in this book relate to situations between players of similar standards. If there is a wide discrepancy between the two, tactics will scarcely matter to the superior and not greatly affect the chances of the inferior. Good tactics will win him more points or games than bad ones and, perhaps, give him a better chance of learning more about tennis. His priority task once the match ends must be to improve technically so that he can effectively turn tactical theory into practice next time he mets the same opponent.

Returning to traffic light tennis, how high over the net to hit the ball from the 'red' zone? If your opponent is also back, why run any risk at all? Two or three feet affords a good safety margin and also helps length, a valuable asset even in these days of serve–volley excesses.

If your opponent is at the net the ball must be kept lower but this can be achieved by use of top spin, which we will analyse later.

Strokes made from the amber zone should normally be played lower over the net than two feet, but not as much lower as you might imagine. Analyses I have made of many matches reveal that all but a handful of shots in any match clear the net by at least a foot, so a foot to eighteen inches can be taken as a working average.

Even from the green zone there is more room above the net than you might think. Because the distance between you and your opponent is greatly reduced, use of controlling top spin or roll to make the ball dip in flight is not going to lessen significantly your chances of putting it beyond his reach. There are so many variables to be considered that no hard and fast rules can be prescribed for any of the zones.

Simply as a rough working guide, treat each return on its merits and remember there is a bigger safety margin over the

35

net than is generally realised. Britain's between-the-Wars 'great' Bunny Austin (he twice ranked second in the world) hardly ever netted, largely because his father chanted at him throughout his childhood that rule already mentioned: 'The main and primary object of the game of lawn tennis is to hit the ball over the net.' Half a dozen infuriating repetitions of this during the first three or four games were remarkably effective in reducing subsequent nettings. And all tactics must begin with the resolve never to give your opponent a cheap point.

Arthur Roberts of Torquay is one of the most successful coaches in the world, especially of women. He advocates:

> length with pace,
> if possible with grace,
> but always length
> with pace.

Next time you have the opportunity to watch women's singles, draw a rough plan of a court on a sheet of paper and put a dot to show where each shot pitches. I warrant that 75 per cent or more will fall in a circle not greater than two yards in radius centred on the junction of the centre and service lines. I did this during a British Hard Court Championship semi-final between Angela Mortimer and Shirley Brasher when both were world 'top-tenners'. Over 90 per cent of Mrs. Brasher's returns pitched in that circle. And, remember, this was a very late stage in the second most important championship in this country.

Each side of a tennis court covers 117 square yards. Restricting yourself to that two yards radius means the use of less than 13 square yards of that area, or little more than 10 per cent. Over 100 square yards of waste. How stupid.

In the first match I have cited, the reason was partly the length of Miss Mortimer's drives. Most women would be satisfied if they could consistently hit within four feet of the baseline. During her Wimbledon-winning era Miss Mortimer pitched ball after ball within four inches of the baseline, and one of the sidelines, thus making life dangerous for anyone who sought to volley her returns rather than allow herself to be forced well behind the baseline by their length.

Length is obtained by giving the ball plenty of 'air'. Three or four feet over the net is commonplace but that is a nice height for volleyers.

However, if your length is as consistently good as Miss Mortimer's (now Mrs. John Barrett) was in her prime, no woman is going to find it easy ever to reach a sound volleying position against you. And if you are a man involved in modern serve–volley matches you will still be surprised how valuable length can be.

In the case of Mrs. Brasher, the length and penetration of Miss Mortimer's ground shots seriously lessened her ability to counter attack and so led to her using that meagre 11 per cent of Miss Mortimer's court.

So cultivate length by constantly practising with a string stretched across the court four feet from the baseline. Play games with your practice opponents in which each shot pitching in that narrow strip counts one and all errors and winners are disregarded.

No player can eliminate all danger of being attacked but consistent length is very sound insurance. Especially, it reduces the angles offered to your opponent.

Figure 3.1 illustrates the truth of this though the actual angles open from the deep, mid and short court positions are, in play, acuter than those shown. This is brought about by the improved safety factor and the greater height at which the ball can often be taken.

Use of top spin also opens up the angles because the ball dips suddenly, lessening the distance between the strike and pitch of the ball. Diagram 3.1 suggests it is difficult to hit a fast drive much shorter in length than the service line. Top spin makes it possible to reduce this distance between hit and pitch. In the diagram the distance from S to the sideline along S_1 is roughly 31 feet. Along the line ST it is approximately 24 feet but the distance along a projection of the baseline to the point where the ball crosses it is considerably increased. This immediately improves the chances of evading your opponent. In the long term it makes him run farther and so use up a great deal more energy.

Again, this is not shown adequately by the diagram. A top spin drive will cause an untouched ball to bound to somewhere around the spot marked 2B. So the opponent will be forced to run diagonally forward. If your next stroke pitches the ball at A

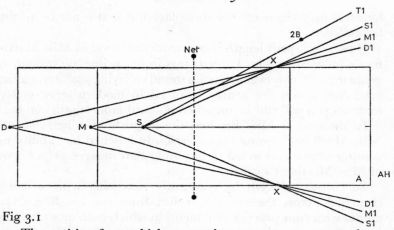

Fig 3.1

The position from which you make your return governs the angles open to you. Assuming X equals the shortest length drive you can make, the angles open to you from D (deep), M (mid court) or S (short) are shown by the projections D1, M1 and S1. In play the gain is better than the geometry shown in this diagram.

he will be forced to hurry back along another diagonal to AH to make his stroke. This lessens his chance of seeing what you are doing unless he ignores the ball and watches you, in which case his chances of making a mistake are greatly increased. Even if he does watch the ball instead of you, the direction of his run will so affect his body position that he will be more liable technically to miss. And even if he does not miss, you can glide quietly and unseen up-court, there to volley his return back along the line ST_1.

Your move up-court will measure about 28 feet so that you will cut twice that distance off the distance the ball travels: 28 feet less to you plus 28 feet less back to him. The total distance from AH to S is around 50 feet so in saving 56 feet by moving up-court to volley you are more than halving the time your opponent has, assuming a rally of constant speed shots.

That is why net attacks behind a short, angled drive followed by a deep approach shot to the opposite sideline are so damaging to the opponent's stamina, especially in women's tennis.

However, angled drives not only open up your opponent's

38

court, they also open up your own. The theory of court positioning after making an angled stroke is simple. You quickly calculate mentally the extent of the angle open to him and then
move to bisect it.

In play it is not so simple. He (or you) may be hurrying un-
duly or worrying excessively or tiring unbearably. In any or all
of these cases he is unusually liable not to direct the ball in any
of the obvious directions. In these situations you (or he) will be
in the superior position and, although you may lose a few points,
you will win a great many more. You will need to be especially
wary on key points because the familiar 'fight or flight' syndrome will momentarily overcome his immediate deficiencies.
At other stages of the match his inferior mental or physical
situation will not be cancelled by the adrenalin flow and you
will retain the percentage chance of winning any given exchange
of angled subtleties.

What happens, however, when you move up a class or two?
The man or woman *en route* to a world top-ten ranking will,
consciously or subconsciously, realise the tendencies and so be
learning to avoid the traps. Though his lungs may be bursting,
his legs torturing him or his brain panic-stricken, self-discipline
is liable to keep him mentally detached. So he will force himself
to run a little faster or longer, to think instead of hitting thought-
lessly. Any series of angle exchanges, therefore, at this level of
tennis is unlikely to follow a predictable pattern.

If you are the man or woman with a mind striving for the top
rungs, you will be the one who decides to continue the angles or
to break the exchanges with a down-the-line shot. In a nut-
shell, this, like so many situations in tennis, is a battle of will and
mind rather than strokes.

Are you tough enough mentally to engage in such battles? If
not now, will you ever be? These are questions to be discussed
later. For now, examine the situation if, through tiredness or
fear, you break up a rally of angled drives.

There is one other relevant point: cross-court returns pass the
net near its lowest height, three feet; down-the-line returns
cross the net nearer its highest point, three feet six inches. That
six inches is all too often the difference between an error and a
continuing rally.

Diagram 3.2 shows very clearly why it is impossible to dog-matise about cross-court rallies.

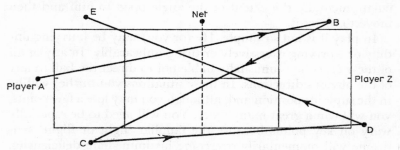

Figure 3.2

Player A hits a cross-court forehand which Z takes at B and returns cross court to C. A has quickly to decide if the gap down the line to D is sufficient for a winner. Since Z will be running back to the centre of the baseline, the down-the line shot will be travelling towards Z. If it does not win the point, Z will be presented with a very wide angle to E and A will have to make a fast 14 yards or so sprint to reach the ball.

So continuously every cross-court rally entails a choice be-tween going for a down-the-line winner or a temporising cross-court return. This choice will be affected by factors such as technical strengths and weaknesses, stamina, nerve and patience. Perhaps above all by speed of foot.

There is only one over-riding rule. It is to dictate to the ball and not to let it dictate to you because of one or more of the factors discussed. This, like all tennis situations between men or women of comparable talents, is 80 per cent a battle of will-power and determination and only 20 per cent one of strokes.

If you are Z and hurrying from B to D, a vital technical point arises which accounts for dozens of apparently needless errors in any match. Your run is taking your body weight out of the stroke instead of into it. In other words your weight is going backwards and your racket swing is deprived of considerable mass. This demands compensation. The best way of achieving this is by stressing and extending the power and length of your follow-through. Use your arm and racket to force the ball away from you. And remember the dangers of netting the ball so give your shot adequate altitude.

Baseline Play

You will not be able to watch the ball *and* your opponent, so you will not know if he has moved in to the net. If you suspect he has, lob; either to the backhand corner or straight down the line to the forehand corner. Most good players are adept at smashing lobs to the backhand corner but many are uncertain when they have to run to the forehand, so try a few down the line.

But whether down the line or across to the backhand, lob over the baseline rather than short, for nothing feeds an opponent's confidence more effectively than a series of short lobs which he can kill with crowd-pleasing flourish and finality. And, please, as soon as you lob, scurry back into position. Assume your lob will be good. Never wait to see if it will be before recovering court position.

Lobs can and should be used defensively for they force your opponent to make positive shots and also give you time to recover court position.

The vital points about defensive lobs are height and depth. The higher you hit the ball, the nearer it will be to the perpendicular when it nears the end of its fall. Additionally, the pull of gravity will be constantly increasing its velocity.

So the volleyer has to strike a ball which is travelling fast in a direction at right angles to the one in which he intends to hit it. This is far from easy, especially if he is at all nervous or apprehensive. On the other hand, there is no chance of your winning the point because he cannot reach the ball, as is the case with a faster, lower lob which is marginally beyond the reach of his racket. The chance of his catching the ball after it has bounced will be lessened even more if you have applied top spin because this causes the ball to race away in a kangaroo-like bound once it touches the ground.

The effect of varying types of lob can be seen in diagram 3.3. The low lob line shows clearly that if you are on the baseline and hit the ball so that the highest point of the arc of its travel is exactly above the net, the ball will land on the opposite baseline.

This gives the clue to successful lobbing: forget the volleyer and think only of your own court position relative to the net. This is the simple system of gunnery: what goes up must come down (unless it is travelling at 'escape' velocity).

Baseline Play

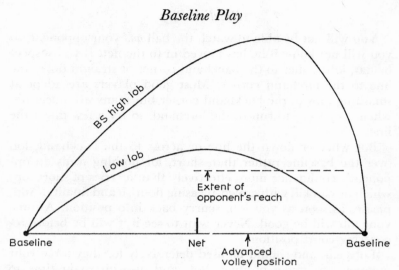

Figure 3.3

The line of the low lob shows an attacking lob which is very useful against a man in the advanced lobbing position who is expecting a passing shot. If you surprise him he will seldom catch the ball. If you do not, the ball will be travelling almost horizontally and so will be easy to kill.

The BS (back spin) high lob will not be uncatchable but at the moment of impact the ball will be dropping almost vertically. Hit high enough and to the full length of the court, the ball will be difficult to kill outright.

In lobbing remember the simple equation for a parabola, $y = x^2$–or, what goes up must come down. So with a flat lob forget the volleyer and all else, and remember only to hit the ball so that the highest point of the arc is exactly over the net.

Hit this way from the baseline on a windless day, the ball will land plumb on the far baseline. The day I discovered this, I hit almost twenty lobs against F. H. D. Wilde in the North of England Championships. All fell right on the baseline, a feat which made *Daily Mail* headlines, surely the only time the lob has reached national paper headlines.

When using this simple system on windy days, one soon earns how to compensate.

The high lob with back spin does not surprise but it can be difficult to kill.

Since length is so crucial when lobbing, think about this example of Pythagoras:

$$\sqrt[2]{78^2+27^2}=82\tfrac{1}{2} \text{ approx.}$$

In tennis terms, you have an extra $4\tfrac{1}{2}$ feet if you lob diagonally from corner to corner instead of straight down the court. This is of prime importance when lobbing defensively. However, in lobbing as in all else, stereotyped methods eventually rebound on the man or woman who perpetrates them. Surprise is the essence of success.

Nevertheless, surprise is not the only thing that counts. Even if the opponent knows in advance that a lob is coming, there can still be a valid reason for using it, as Drobny proved on several occasions when beating Frank Sedgman. Sedgman was phenomenally quick and in the early stages of any match was virtually impossible to pass at the net. How long he stayed at top speed related directly to the length of time he retained his starting freshness. So whenever they met, Drobny lobbed non-stop for one set even though he knew he would lose it. The gambit was necessary because only by continually forcing Sedgman to smash could he erode Sedgman's peak freshness; later, his net-covering capabilities reduced sufficiently for Drobny to have room for passing shots.

The 1952 final of the British Hard Court Championships at Bournemouth provided a classic example for, so accurate were Drobny's early lobs, he even won the first set before taking the final 6–2, 6–4, 1–6, 6–4. Though Sedgman was unquestionably the most agile and destructive volleyer of the day, his margin of winning points over losses in the second, third and fourth sets was plus 12. Over the same period Drobny's tally was plus 15.

That is the measure of how skilful lobbing destroyed the man who was to win the Wimbledon singles two months later.

So abandon all thoughts that the lob is merely a defensive stroke and consider it instead as a valuable attacking or, if you prefer, counter-attacking weapon in your stroke armoury.

Drop shots are more obviously attacking weapons than lobs. Yet they are used in a defensive situation more often than is generally realised, maybe because the defensive aspect is too subtle for simple recognition.

A drop shot is one played to drop the ball just over the net, either to win the point outright or to bring the opponent racing up-court to scramble the ball over the net from a court position leaving vast gaps for a placement. It sounds a delicate shot and to some degree this is so. Because of this the natural tendency is to attempt it off a falling ball. This means the ball is normally struck from below the level of the net. Backspin is applied to prevent the ball bounding forward but the ball still has to be hit upwards. Thus the bounce tends to be higher than necessary, the safety margin is not high and the time delay between strike and bounce is normally sufficient to allow an active opponent to reach the ball in some comfort.

That is the common way of making a drop shot. It is not the method of Jaroslav Drobny, possibly the best maker of the stroke in the history of tennis. He makes the stroke positively and in an aggressive state of mind. Instead of waiting for the ball to pass the top of its bounce, he moves forward to play it just at or before this high point in its travel. So he gains in two ways: he takes the ball several feet nearer to the net than the usual player; the trajectory of the ball after he has struck it will be much flatter so that it will not bounce so high after hitting the ground.

Drop shots are normally hit straight ahead rather than across the court. Depending on how good it is and on the mobility of the opponent, after making a drop shot you should either move a few steps forward or else remain back and in a state of alertness to move in any direction.

If you have played the stroke off a rising ball you will be forward anyway. Often you will be able to volley your opponent's return, perhaps in a lob over his head to the baseline. I have seen Drobny tear the lungs out of his opponents with successions of dropshot–lob–dropshot–lob.

Your best answer to a drop shot is almost entirely dependent on your quickness in spotting it and speed in reaching the ball. This, like so many facets of tennis, suggests that speed of reflex and movement is the most important asset one can possess.

If you reach the ball in any comfort you will be on balance and in a reasonably favourable forward position on the court.

44

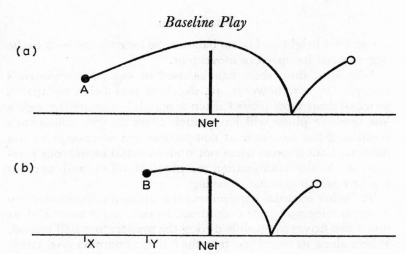

Figure 3.4

In (a) the drop shot is struck from below net level. Even with back spin the ball has to be hit higher over the net than in (b) so that it will tend to land farther away from the net than in (b) and so bounce higher and in a slightly greater forward angle.

In (b) the ball is struck at net height so it need not be lifted so much. It can be made to bounce nearer the net, less high than in (a) and in a slightly more perpendicular manner because the back spin will have had less time to slow down.

Notice, too, that the opponent's return will not have been allowed to travel from Y to X; nor will the ball have to travel back from X to Y. The saving in time can be considerable, certainly sufficient to make the difference between a winning and an ordinary shot.

But taking the ball on the rise or at the top of its bounce demands an aggressive attitude, from which it follows that drop shots, though soft, are undeniably attacking ones.

Because time is vital they should generally be made straight ahead; the ball takes longer to travel across the court than straight down it.

On the other hand, if you just reach the ball and are off balance, you will be in no state to make a good reply or to recover balance before racing after the ensuing shot.

Theoretically an answering drop shot is probably the best riposte but to make a good drop shot you need to stroke the ball

45

around net height and be on balance. So here we are back to the urgent need for speed of movement.

Like lobs, drop shots can be used to sap your opponent's energy. Do not, however, be deceived into believing that a series of drop shots played when a match is passing through a low pressure phase will have much effect on your opponent's stamina. Most tournament competitors are fit enough to run miles without distress when not under mental or nervous pressure. It is the combination of physical effort and nervous pressure which gets men gasping.

The other essential requirement is a modicum of surprise. Try never to telegraph your drop shots. In fact, make them look as much like drives as possible during the preparatory half second. Where along its travel you take the ball is a common give-away. Hitting the ball on the rise renders 'reading' your strokes more difficult than when you allow it to fall.

Do not over-use drop shots; rather deploy them as yet another way of exploiting geometrically the 117 square yards of court across the net.

All this presupposes that all your opponents will dislike hitting the ball on the run. This is not always so. Many, especially those with a long swing, are unhappy and uncertain when each ball is hit straight at them. This may be because of technical deficiencies or simply because their ability to make their own angles is limited. Louise Brough gave a classic display of refusing to open up angles when returning every ball straight to Beverly Fleitz while winning the 1955 Wimbledon final.

Left-handers, too, have an advantage in this respect: their forehand drives, viewed from behind, normally swing the ball from left to right, that is, into a right-hander's forehand. And there are very few right-handers who are happy with shots that swing into their elbows. This is equally true of left-handed services and it was always the profitable policy of Rod Laver to serve many in-swingers to Ken Rosewall in their frequent battles of the late 1960s.

Many players, especially nervous ones, prefer to be made to run when attempting to pass volleyers at the net; it is almost as if the effort of running reduces their tension, enabling them to strike the ball more freely. Manuel Santana used this effectively in many of his skilful encounters with Nicola Pietrangeli who disliked having to wait for the ball to come down to him.

Similarly, nineteen players out of twenty are happier running from side to side and back again across the baseline than they are when forced to run from side to side and then to turn and go back to the side they have just left. Angela Buxton had never won more than three games in a set from Pat Ward, nor Christine Truman more than three from Ann Shilcock, until they were told to play rigidly forehand–backhand–backhand or backhand–forehand–forehand. These simple tactics enabled both to win with relative ease, an amazing turn-round in either case.

Moving a player up and down the court is another potential gatherer of points from errors. A deep drive followed by a half pace fade or slice to the forehand usually exposes any uncertainty in an opponent's forehand. One can sometimes judge this by the opponent's grip before he even hits the ball, for if his hand is farther behind the racket than in a normal Eastern grip, he is liable to have difficulty in moving forward to slow returns directed to his forehand. Mervyn Rose used this system to beat defending champion Dick Savitt in the 1952 Wimbledon singles. Again, sometimes one can discern an opponent's weaknesses of movement during the knock-up. Better, though, to watch him in an earlier match.

Hitting to a weakness demands slightly more subtlety. Theoretically a weakness should be pulverised into destruction. In practice this does not always happen.

Much depends on the form of weakness. Christine Janes's heavily dragged backhand was so fundamentally incorrect that it was virtually incapable of being worked into a strength in the short space of one three-set match. Thus it was generally safe to pound away at it indiscriminately. There were, however, a few matches during her career in which, out of sheer desperation, she began lobbing everything off that wing. On one or two occasions she lobbed so well that she beat opponents who were expected to win. If they had been more discriminating she might never have switched to tactics which ultimately proved successful.

Jean Borotra did not fall into this trap during one of his many matches with René Lacoste.[1] Lacoste developed one of the

[1] *Lacoste on Tennis* by René Lacoste.

strongest backhands in tennis history but on this particular day it was not functioning well. Borotra, one of the most intelligent men of his era, reasoned that if he concentrated on that backhand Lacoste would work it back into its usual stonewall groove. So he held his serve as best he could up to four-all in each of the first two sets before making a series of quick net sorties on that backhand to secure his service break. Leaving the backhand severely alone, he lost the third and fourth sets and then, when there was insufficient time remaining for Lacoste to groove the shot, he unleashed an all-out attack which captured the set and the match.

Here it is as well to emphasise what is meant by attacking a weakness. It does not mean simply hitting the ball to that weakness and hoping for mistakes. Attacking implies working on a weakness until its owner is completely destroyed. If the weakness is an inability in the player to make his own pace, then he is seldom or never fed with a fast drive. If high-kicking serves are anathema to him, then high-kickers followed to the net are fed in profusion; the policy is similar if slices or top spins cause difficulty, then they are used in abundance.

The routine, therefore, is to feed the right–or wrong?–kind of shot or series of shots to the weakness and to force your opponent to do something positive with a return. Maybe you will force him to make a passing shot or perhaps generate his own pace. If he is incapable of hitting the ball down the line, you will cover the cross-court so completely that you will force him to try for down the line; *vice versa* if cross-court is his weakness.

Some men are so skilled in defending their weakness or even using it at all that one is virtually forced to hit first to the strength in order to expose the weakness. The late George Godsell, a successful English tournament player, was one such player. Very adept at running round the first shot of any rally hit to his backhand, he had first to be dragged right across the court to the forehand and the next ball driven or volleyed to his now exposed backhand. But as his first forehand return was usually very strong, it was necessary to be very alert in order to hit an effective shot to the now open backhand. The opener to the forehand had to be an attacking shot–not a ball hit there hopefully–and it was still necessary to be very alert for a powerful return. It was no situation for a mental dullard. At a higher level, Christine Janes was very susceptible to this routine, especially against Lesley Bowrey.

Conversely, it was certain destruction to use the 'attack the strength to expose the weakness' routine against Pancho Segura. He kept both hands on his racket handle and hit this type of forehand so severely, deceptively and accurately that the chances of ever getting to the weakness second time were very remote. So no matter how narrow the gap, the first shot had to be aimed at the weakness and the strength attacked only when the odds favoured an outright winner. His forehand, like that of many others, was vulnerable to a backhand fader down the sideline.

This useful shot is mid-way between a drive and a drop shot in pace, is pitched a yard or so short of the service line and with sufficient slide–slice imparted by hitting through the ball instead of by dragging the racket under, so causing it to sit up–to make the ball lie down after bouncing. This is a most useful weapon which should be developed early in one's competitive career.

There is one trap which must always be avoided: trying to outdrive an opponent who is fundamentally a more severe, more consistent and more accurate hitter of groundstrokes than you. To this end you should discover the optimum speed of your drives. That is a speed above which your errors increase sharply while by dropping below it your mistakes scarcely show any reduction. Having discovered this optimum speed, seek to increase it on the practice court, perhaps by constantly taking the ball a little nearer to the spot where it bounces. This is a lengthy and arduous process and if you can move forward six inches a year for your average shots you will not be doing at all badly.

Optimum speed can also be increased by improving your techniques of stroke play–but that is scarcely a subject for this book. A reminder about hitting through the ball so as to hold it on the racket strings a fraction longer is, perhaps, in order.

To return to the matter of trying to outdrive a fundamentally superior stroke maker–how can you tell for sure? Apart from the score–1–6 is a pretty strong indication–an alert player should be able to feel such a situation in his bones. If your opponent is in a higher class than you, your change of tactics may not prove fruitful. Yet the change must be theoretically correct and, therefore, an aid to subsequent advance even if not a match winner at the moment.

In this situation recall the 'traffic signal' system outlined earlier. Do not feed him with pace. Give the ball plenty of air. Vary the pace of your drives, not so markedly that a blind man could see it but fractionally so that your opponent may be deceived. Do not fall into the common error of hitting the ball too hard when you are being run into a state of breathlessness. One runs and hits hard in the hope of ending the rally. Do not do it. Keep your mind detached, play a safe shot—possibly a lob to the backhand corner—and be prepared to hit another twenty shots in the rally if necessary. Never give up mentally by attempting an 'against the odds' shot simply to end a torturing rally or because you are frightened at the way it is developing. Tennis matches are won by mental toughness, by 'staying' with your opponent until he virtually breaks under the strain.

It is possible to help this process along by discovering his pet shots early on and then deliberately letting him win a few points with them. Later in the match you can lower his morale by feeding those same shots but moving to the correct position to score with counter-attacks. Unless he is very astute he will not realise the trap you have laid though he may still hit shots good enough to win the points. But if he does not, you may well increase any feeling he has that you have contained his game and that he has no way of breaking free.

There is one other point to remember in baseline play and that is the stage in its flight where you actually hit the ball. Once it was fashionable to stroke every ball before it reached the top of its bounce. Today a close analysis reveals that even Rod Laver plays three-quarters of his shots off balls that have just passed the top of the bounce and are beginning to fall. He saves the other quarter for attack when the opportunity arises or counter-attack when forced to do so. In this way he follows what is probably the most important axiom for any type of play: the 'treat each ball on its merits' rule. Learn to judge accurately the merit of each ball hit to you and how best to treat it; then the rallies, points, games, sets and matches will slowly take care of themselves.

4 · Net Play

Analyse any Wimbledon, American or Australian champion-ship late-stage men's singles of recent years and you will discover that nine points out of ten end with one man either making for or at the net, though there is nothing new about net play. The never-ending battle between volleyer and baseliner began early in tennis history. Spencer Gore, the first Wimbledon champion, overcame his opponents by following deep drives to the net and there volleying the ball first here, then there, by 'a dexterous turn of the wrist', to quote T. G. Heathcote, his semi-final victim. One year later he lost to P. F. Hadow who neutralised his net game by the simple tactic of lobbing the ball over his head for it to fall near the baseline.

There are six vital elements in successful net play: daring, surprise, depth, speed and decision on the volley and singleness of purpose. They are all inter-related.

There can be no half measures, no lack of conviction when you go to the net. You are in an advanced position where you can be easily passed by a fast shot to either side line so it is entirely a case of the survival of the fittest. This does not imply, however, that you can or should rush the net behind every single service or shot you make. That would be to invite extinc-tion against any opponent worth his salt.

On the other hand, wooden surface courts are non-resistant to the ball; grass, especially of Wimbledon standard, is very similar to wood in its playing qualities. Thus a baseliner has to hit his returns along an upward plane and has far less time to make them than on red clay courts. On grass or wood, or polished cement, take advantage of this by attacking from the net far more frequently than on clay.

You must think of the net position as one where you finish rallies, even on clay and slower surfaces. The difference is that you have to be more patient in creating the right moments for net attacks on clay. Depth, both of service and approach shot, is important and, ideally, your balance should be superior to your opponent's on each approach that you make.

Balance is affected by the foothold of the court and your own nimbleness. If you are a naturally agile 'slider' you will be undisturbed by a slippery clay court. So you will not be inhibited from going to the net through fear of falling. I am six feet one inch tall and was always frozen solid by slippery clay; on the other hand, I held the advantage over those who liked sliding when playing on firm surfaces. Such considerations are relevant even if they are often 75 per cent psychological rather than actual. If the opponent is more agile than you, you will have to be more sure than at other times in making your advance. Especially, you must guard against being surprised.

Whether or not you are nimble, you are likely to fall into the common danger of fearing the lob. This will make you hold back fractionally, thus making it easier for your opponent to pass you, catch you at your feet or force you into a weak reply by tipping the ball low and at half pace to either sideline.

Learn, therefore, to scorn the lob; develop a powerful overhead kill and a speed when running backwards nearly equal to your forward speed. This demands intensive, purposeful training; but Borotra in the '20s, Sedgman in the '50s and Laver in the '60s proved that it can be done. When practising net advances in particular, refrain from checking your run-in at the moment your opponent hits the ball. This is done by ninety-nine out of a hundred players in match play and you will probably remain one of the ninety-nine. The idea of the pause is to steady balance and be in an alert state of readiness to spring in any direction.

You should strive through the speed of your run-in to be further forward than average when balancing to jump in any way directed by your opponent's shot. It is even better if you can learn to change direction while still running. But if you cannot, practising a quicker run-in will soon have you one, two and possibly three paces nearer the net before pausing. And two paces farther forward can mean winning half a dozen extra points a match; this is often more than the margin between defeat and victory.

Training—the intensive training that hurts and hurts—will

gradually increase your speed at the net and in getting back from the net to kill lobs. This is important because, in keeping with the primitive 'him or me' philosophy of successful net play, you must develop a complete scorn for the lob. This scorn goes beyond the knowledge that, no matter what happens, you can get back to the ball. It demands a positive attitude which tells you 'my point' whenever you see a lob leave your opponent's racket.

There are several good reasons why an attitude of scorning the lob and closing right in to the net is not quite as dangerous as it may seem. Your side of the court measures 13 yards in depth. If advancing five yards forward brings one degree of danger, it might seem that advancing 10 yards would involve two degrees of danger. In fact, this is not the case.

The training which enables you to reach a more advanced position will have improved your technical efficiency and skills; this alone will enable you to reach as many wide shots as you did in your pre-training days of volleying from a greater distance from the net.

Your volleys from nearer the net open up wider angles, enabling you to take the ball above the net instead of below it and so will be far more decisive. This, apart from its direct point-winning aspect, wins many points by frightening your opponent into mistakes.

Study the statistics of ten men's singles and you will find that 60 per cent of the points are won through unforced errors. For a classic example I recall two singles between M. D. Deloford and A. G. Roberts at an immediately post-war Wimbledon. They drew each other in the first round, and played an orthodox match which Roberts won; Roberts lost his second-round match and, by a strange coincidence, drew to play Deloford in the All England Plate. Realising from the first match that his fitness could not sustain orthodoxy, Deloford decided that this time he would rush the net on everything. Afterwards he said, 'I only made two volleys in three sets and they were both losers.' For the rest of the time Roberts either passed him cleanly or made mistakes. In fact, his mistakes were so numerous that a net attack which produced only volley errors nevertheless won the match for Deloford. Roberts was pressurised into making errors when they were unnecessary, as so often happens when a volleyer meets a baseliner.

Bear in mind, too, that the pressure is cumulative: your opponent may pass you easily in the first set but he will find the task increasingly difficult as the match progresses and by the end of the final set the odds will have swung sharply in your favour.

This links with the other great advantages gained by developing the speed of foot and thought which make possible a close-in volleying position. At the same time you develop an adventurous outlook which generates optimism and the will to command success.

This contrasts with the inherently safer outlook of the man who attempts to defend from the baseline. A safety first approach tends to compress the personality and this is one of the dangers of 'playing the percentages' which is so popular today. There are moments every year when you have to stake all your tennis chips on one brisk gamble and this puts immense premiums on confidence and speed.

There is another factor which I have already dealt with in the previous chapter. I think that it bears repetition. When danger threatens—and who can deny the dangers of a forward volleying position except when dealing with a sitter?—the adrenal gland pumps adrenalin into the system and this speeds reaction time and subsequent movement. This, perhaps more than anything, accounts for the many superb shots on set and match points in big matches. When technique and a sense of adventure are linked together, as they are supremely in Rod Laver, you find a truly great player—in Laver's case probably the greatest ever.

All this detail should have persuaded you of the necessity to train like a fanatic in order to become an 'advanced position' volleyer.

You should also develop techniques which make your approaches more likely to win points. If you are a powerful ground stroke player in the mould of Donald Budge or, lower down the scale, Bob Hewitt, most of your net advances will be to deal with weak returns. If your ground strokes are less powerful or sure, greater demands will be made on your agility and actual prowess on the volley. In the former case, you advance with the near certain knowledge of winning the point; in the latter you have first to reach the net without being passed or forced into a mistake. Having reached the net in safety, you then have usually to force a winner off a difficult return with your volley. Since the techniques for either case are the same we need only discuss net approaches for the latter.

In terms of angles, the safest approach is behind a deep drive to the middle of your opponent's court. As this removes any necessity for him to hit the ball on the run, he can choose whether to use his forehand or backhand, and he is centrally positioned to run down your volley. Hence your volley must carry more penetration than when there is a gaping hole for the placement. On the other hand, there are a number of players who prefer to hit their passing shots on the run. The Italian ace Nicola Pietrangeli is an example from the highest class; in women's tennis, the great tactician Ann Jones is more dangerous counter-hitting on the run against a volley than she is when the ball is floated deep to her backhand, though that method is no guarantee of success against her.

The preliminary to any successful net campaign is to discover what your opponent likes and dislikes when making his passing shots. Try him out in four ways:

Approach behind a deep drive to the centre of his baseline;
Hit the ball from sideline to sideline and move in when you have got him well on the run;
Make him turn during the rally by hitting the ball, say, right-left-right-right, and go in on the shot where he has to turn back to the side he has just left;
Take his service on the rise and push it deep to the backhand or straight at him.

This should reveal any preference he has for hitting on the run or when stationary and for hitting when running from side to side or when made to turn in mid-course.

If you are ambitious and meticulous enough to become a champion, you will have discovered these facts by studying your opponent in previous matches and noted down all your findings in a book. Use a loose-leaf file because you will wish to add further details as you progress.

There is no hard and fast rule about what you will discover but, probably, he will be least happy when made to hit after turning and very often when turning to the forehand. Despite popular ideas, the forehand is technically a more difficult stroke than the backhand and many players are discomfited when they hit a forehand, run for the middle of the baseline and then have to turn back to hit another forehand.

This raises another important *caveat* in net play: learn to be equally at home volleying returns from all directions, forehand, backhand or centre.

The body balance for these returns is not constant. Nor are the angles of play and sight. Jaroslav Drobny, Wimbledon champion in 1954 and one of the greatest clay court players, has written many times in *Lawn Tennis* magazine that he nearly always went to the net behind shots to his opponent's backhand, even when it was far stronger than the forehand, simply because he felt better balanced and able to anticipate the direction of returns from the backhand than from the forehand. He also admits this was a slight deficiency in his game.

Such weaknesses derive from habits acquired early in one's career. They can easily be avoided simply by attacking opponents' forehands when they are men who can be beaten with a fair degree of certainty. It is a matter of mental discipline rather than technique. If you lack mental discipline you are unlikely to achieve even your simplest ambitions.

All these, however, may be classified as simple approaches and in advanced levels of tennis they are unlikely to hurt opponents on the points which matter most. Thus more skilled approaches have to be acquired and mastered.

Figure 4.1 shows a very practical and useful sequence, especially in women's tennis. It was used to telling and devastating effect by Jack Kramer in his halcyon days when serving in the right court. He would swerve and slice the ball viciously out to the forehand sideline, so taking his opponent beyond the sidelines and a yard or two up-court towards the net. Kramer's next return would travel fast and low to the backhand corner, and he would follow it in to the net. If his opponent reached the ball and got it back the odds were twenty to one on Kramer's

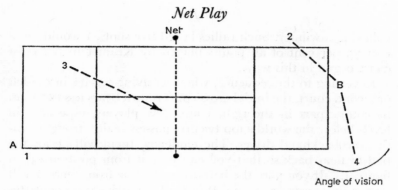

Figure 4.1

You are A receiving service from B who does not follow service to the net on this occasion. You return the service from (1) across court to (2) forcing B to run diagonally forwards. Frequently he will aim for your backhand so that on many occasions you will be able to play your second shot from position (3). Meanwhile he will begin to hurry back to the centre of the baseline.

If your next shot is deep to the backhand so that he takes the ball at (4) his angle of vision will not permit him both to watch the ball and to keep a fraction of his sight on you. If you, therefore, move in to the net, he must either guess your court position or take his eye off the ball. If you have studied him carefully in previous matches you should know his tendencies seven or more times out of ten and so be in position for a winning volley into the gap. Once he starts watching you instead of the ball his errors will rise significantly.

The danger of this sequence lies in your first cross-court return. It must pitch near to the sideline and, preferably, carry top spin so that he is driven well out of court. If it does not, he will be able to play the ball down the backhand line and move in. But even if he does, your run will be straight along the baseline instead of diagonally backwards, so that you will have a reasonable idea of his court position. Additionally, the line of the ball brings it towards you. When you hit to position 4 from 3, the ball runs away from him.

This particular sequence can be used more often in women's singles than men's. It can be used in reverse from the backhand court, your first return being short and cross-court to his backhand and your following shot deep to the forehand or, to keep him guessing, occasionally deep to the backhand.

volleying a winner. Such rallies lasted five shots. I would guess that 75 per cent of all points played by Kramer in the right court began in this way.

Reverting to the sequence, when receiving service in the left or second court, the initial cross-court return bears less risk than its counterpart in the right court; few players, especially in levels below the world's top twenty, possess really strong down-the-line backhand drives. The tendency, then, will be for the ball to float back so that you can play it from position (3) in figure 4.1. If you play the ball down the line from there it will be running away from him. If instead you drive cross court towards (4) he will have to turn quite sharply because, almost certainly, he will be scurrying towards the baseline in order to bisect the angle open to your shot. Turning will lessen his chances of throwing body weight into his shot and so it is likely to lack penetration. Usually you will be able to volley the ball beyond his reach but in case of doubt punch it hard towards (4) again. Turning a second time will generally force an even weaker return or an error.

Indeed, so accurate is this observation that it might form a rule: when in doubt, punch the ball hard and deep to the place from which opponent hit his previous shot. Certainly Tony Trabert used this system continually when winning Wimbledon in 1955.

The most vital factor in these short, across court, deep to the opposite corner sequences is the goodness of the first cross-court return. The margin between an effective, court opening return and one which hands the initiative to your opponent on a plate is very slender. Yet it can be a prolific point winner, so every minute of practice spent directing cross-court returns of service to targets placed on or near the respective junctions of service and sidelines is time used to immense advantage.

These sequences are particularly useful on clay courts, especially when your second shot is deep across the court to the backhand, because time and again your opponent will only be able to float the ball back high across the net and vaguely in the direction of your backhand. Most men will be at the net already. Many women will not. Yet whether you are a man or a woman, you should develop a shot which I have yet to see recommended in a text book. This is the volley drive.

Imagine that you have hit short to the forehand, deep to the backhand, remained on the baseline and he has floated back a semi-lob. If you allow the ball to bounce you will have to retreat behind the baseline; he will have ample time to regain position and you will be back to where you started.

Consider, however, the effect if, instead of retreating nine feet, you had run forward nine feet and played exactly the same safe shot but without letting the ball bounce. You would have shortened the ball's travelling distance your side of the net by 18 feet to you and a further 18 feet back to him – 36 feet in all. As a percentage of total distance this is around 25 per cent, or a quarter.

So even if your shot is identical in pace and placement to the ground stroke, you will force your opponent to run one third as fast again as if you had let the ball bounce. His extra effort, multiplied a number of times over two sets, will be worth a feast of points to you in the third set.

Actually, once you forget the silly aura of difficulty given to volley drives, you will be able to make very much more aggressive shots than when you play the same ball as a ground stroke from behind the baseline. So you will both save time, gain angle, and speed. The effect on your opponents will be decisive.

In playing the volley drive, forehand or backhand, merely shorten your swing marginally, watch the ball carefully and strike it confidently.

Add to your general rules the warning: never let a floating return drop; always volley drive it.

Volley drives have to be driven; they cannot effectively be used as drop volleys, that is, volleys which just creep over the net, the ball dying quickly after bouncing. This volley, played from near the net, is very effective when your approach shot has forced your opponent behind his baseline. It is a pleasing shot to play, a crowd pleaser and, like many drugs, is habit-forming. In this it is dangerous.

If you think back to the 'fight or flight' syndrome you will remember how your reactions and movements are speeded up. This works against the man who is 'hooked' on drop volleys.

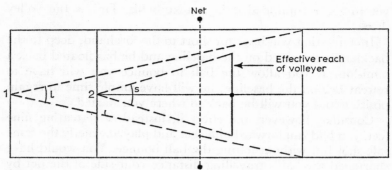

Figure 4.2

Assuming the service line is the shortest length to which you can hit a first drive, a long approach to position (1) leaves room for a fast passing shot to evade the volleyer's effective reach (angle L).

If the approach shot is short and low, forcing the passing shot to be made from position (2), angle *s* shows that a fast passing shot cannot evade the volleyer's racket; if the volleyer is quick-reacting and a rapid mover of the racket (so he is not vulnerable to a short range, fast drive straight at his middle) he will gather a harvest of points.

The defender will have to slow the speed of his passing shots in order to increase the angle *s* and in reducing their speed will improve the volleyer's chances of reaching the ball. By watching Dick Savitt carefully and then using long-short tactics, Mervyn Rose ended Savitt's bid in 1952 to retain the Wimbledon singles title he won in 1951.

Apart from angles, the psychological effect of rushing forward to scrape up a ball while you can see the opponent menacing you from a short distance away is very much in favour of the volleyer.

Early in the match they catch his opponent flat-footed so he is encouraged to persevere with their use. As the match progresses the opponent will learn to anticipate them and react with greater rapidity because of the physiological changes caused by danger. So he will begin to reach the ball, and, because of the range, gain an ascendancy over the volleyer.

The volleyer should realise the danger and switch to deep volleys because depth is a volleyer's trusty friend; all too probably, however, he will have become 'hooked' and thus unable to stop himself from using drop volleys. In order to win points he will try to drop the ball ever nearer the net, errors will creep in and his net attacks will tend to become point losers where once they were winners. Drop volleys are invaluable. They are also insidious. By all means use them but always keep them in control and subservient to depth and pace.

There is one other very effective way of beating a strong ground-stroke player by volleying: by reversing the usual short–long approach. You hit the ball deep, slice the second shot short and low and rush to the net behind it. Figure 4.2 shows the geometry of this sequence.

The final point to be made about volleying is the necessity of thinking positively—of not being discouraged by a few shots that speed by beyond your reach but, instead, pushing home your net attacks with even greater determination. And, of course, considering your first volley as the shot which ends the rally there and then.

From the other side of the net, really purposeful net attacks have the relentlessness of a strong tide battering on the sea front. You repulse sortie after sortie and still he pounds down on you. He never gives you a moment's respite. Your resolve weakens briefly and he immediately increases the pressure, getting on the ball quicker and forcing you to hurry more and more over your passing shots until you finally crack open. That is the cumulative effect of purposeful volleying. That is why you must master net play and add it to your assets.

5 · Service and Return of Service

There is one stroke on which the opponent can have no effect – at any rate not directly, even if psychologically. So it is entirely up to you to develop your service to a high degree of efficiency with the help of coaching and practice. If you consider that by winning every service game you can never be beaten, every minute spent on service improvement and consolidation must be valuable.

Aces which are so well placed and fast that the receiver cannot get his racket to them are great crowd pleasers: they are very spectacular. And there is enough of the actor in all of us to enjoy enthusiastic applause. Yet speed is by no means the only criterion of good service. Jean Borotra's service was slower than that of many women competing in tournaments today; but it was pitched so consistently within an inch or two of the service line, placed so cunningly, kept so low and hit at an ideal speed to allow him to reach an ideal volleying position that it was extremely difficult to break. Judged on its own as an isolated stroke it was at best moderate; considered as part of Borotra's entire game, it was formidably effective.

Jack Kramer's serving was more powerful than Borotra's but still far less powerful than that of many of his contemporaries, including Gonzales. Gonzales was among many who maintained that Kramer's service was the hardest to break. Like Borotra's it was blended with consummate skill into the rest of his game. Its success was based very largely on his sliced service in the right-hand (first) court. Hitting the ball on its outside, he swerved it sharply from right to left, causing it to pitch near the forehand sideline and so drag the receiver well beyond the sideline. Figure 5.1 shows the sequences which developed.

In the left (second) court Kramer consistently served deep, fast balls to the junction of the service and backhand sidelines, so forcing his opponents back on to their heels. These he generally followed to the net and from there either volleyed the ball

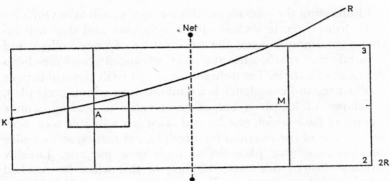

Figure 5.1

Kramer's sliced service in the right court. Hit with spin, the ball swerved sharply so that the usual point of return was somewhere around R but the service always carried quite a lot of pace. So a significant percentage of the service returns landed in the rectangular area A. Then Kramer normally hit a deep drive to (2) while moving to the net. His opponent, forced to run diagonally backwards and fast, hit the ball at such a disadvantage that he seldom won a point.

To keep his opponents guessing Kramer forced a proportion of his second shots to 3, so compelling the receiver to turn rapidly in his swift run to cover the gap. To stop the receiver moving in to receive service, so reducing the distance he was carried beyond the sideline, Kramer interspersed a small proportion of fast services down the middle line to M, which he followed to the net.

On 90 per cent of key points, however, he used the sliced serve-deep approach sequence.

deep back into the backhand corner or sharply across court into the opening. He varied his choice so cleverly that the receiver was never permitted to settle into any comfortable routine.

Here I would like to pinpoint one very common fault of men who consistently follow their services to the net. They serve, run a step or two, hesitate in case it is a fault and then continue their run to the net. If you decide you are going to follow your serve to the net, do so without hesitation. Place up the ball, hit it and light out for the net as fast as you can, completely disregarding any possibility of the service being a fault.

Eliminating the understandable hesitation will take you anything from three to six feet closer to the net and that will increase enormously both the penetration of your volleys and
your effective reach, since the more advanced position reduces
the receiver's angle. The unhesitating run-in will also add to your
confidence, and confidence is a vital factor in winning net play.

Change of length is not of great value in serving, unlike
change of pace which can be and often is a valuable tool. Surprise is one of the essential features of good tactics, so excessive
changes of service pace defeat their own purpose. Jaroslav
Drobny showed full understanding of this when he reached
match point against Ken Rosewall in the 1954 Wimbledon
singles. His tactics have already been fully analysed in Chapter
two; they deserve a second look as they show a highly skilled
use of change of pace.

Rosewall was then fourteen years younger than when he beat
John Newcombe in the 1968 final at Wembley. Obviously, the
years added considerably to Rosewall's experience but Newcombe, though a skilled tactician, does not make extensive use
of changes of service pace. In the Wembley final, which went to
four sets, Rosewall held six breaks altogether. He got the ball
into play on every occasion and won the point five times out of
the six. An exemplary demonstration but one wonders what
might have happened if Newcombe had varied his pace or spin
on one or two of the points. He had a strong service; it com-
pares favourably with Laver's. On those six break points he
served twice to the forehand and four times to the backhand, a
one to two ration. Overall, however, his ratio was 46 forehand,
68 backhand.

When Laver beat Rosewall in the 1968 Wembley final, he
served 30 times to the forehand and 82 to the backhand. But
like most left-handers, he feels more comfortable advancing to
the net on the backhand than on the forehand. So on game
points he served to the backhand 32 times and only tried to
surprise Rosewall on the forehand on five occasions. This revealed an overall strategy to create uncertainty in his opponent,
but his tactics on key points were both orthodox and in accordance with techniques at which he considers himself best.

Because the receiver may, within reason, choose the moment

64

when he wishes to take service, he is less vulnerable to sudden bursts of speed than when hurrying around the court in a rally. Additionally, glandular activity in crises will give him additional sensitivity to violent change.

In general, then, one should endeavour to create surprise stress in his mind over the less crucial stages of a match and play the percentages on key points. However, continual surprise is no surprise at all, and, certainly, anyone who followed the theory of the preceding paragraph to the letter would soon be completely 'read' by even a moderately shrewd competitive player. So even on critical points one should occasionally change pace. But only slightly. Perhaps a slightly faster ball straight at the man, hoping that he is keyed up to spring instantaneously in any direction. The left-hander's inswinger to a right-hander's forehand can be very effective when used sparingly on key points.

Spin, too, can embarrass the receiver. A sliced service to the sideline on the forehand side of a damp court keeps the ball low and is a real worrier. An American twist service kicks the ball sharply away from a right-hander's backhand. If he is unhappy returning the ball when it is rising, such kickers will drive the receiver back and out of court, leaving him vulnerable if you follow service to the net.

On the other hand, if he has quick reflexes, he will move in, take the ball at shoulder height and chop the ball down to your feet as you run in. And if you do not run in his quick reflexes will enable him to spot what is happening, chop the ball back deep and reach the net himself under advantageous conditions. Then it may be that a kicker or two served away to his forehand so that the ball jumps in at him will force a few mistakes.

All these permutations make one special demand: to be more alert than your opponent, especially on key points. These are the occasions when it is dangerous to chance going for an untouchable ace or unreturnable winner. Your second service may be almost as powerful as your first but your opponent seldom or never fears it as much. So when you fault his confidence will rise and, as has been said, confidence is half the battle. He will move in on your second service and make a forcing shot which may well take the initiative away from you.

By and large, therefore, sacrifice the extra 10 per cent of speed which converts fast services into aces, get in a powerful deep ball, and, on a fast court, follow the ball to the net. Direct the serve either to his weaker wing or to the one you find easier to anticipate and volley against. If you are 40/love or 40/15 try, perhaps, for an ace; but only do so at 40/30 as a calculated gamble or if you are very confident. Never make life easy for your opponent on key points. Nothing is more heartening than to be game point down and then have the point presented to you on a plate. Make him work like a fiend, if only because of the cumulative effect this attitude will have on his morale and stamina.

There will inevitably be days when your first serves are so treacherous or ineffective that you simply cannot keep your opponent away from the net. No matter what risks you take, he moves in on the ball, prods it deep in your court and then camps on the net. You should accept that this will happen and try to make his approach to the net as hazardous as possible. Again, sacrifice some speed and serve wide to the two sidelines. Figure 5.2 shows why.

Angela Buxton once lost to Darlene Hard, serving in the normal way. Six weeks later she used this system and completely reversed the result . . . and on a court which favoured Miss Hard's net play.

Most players in singles serve in the right court from a position as near as possible to the midpoint along the baseline; and in the left court from perhaps a yard to the left of this position.

Moving farther to the right along the baseline increases the angle your service can make with the sideline, so driving the receiver wider of the sidelines than when you serve from the centre division. However, this also opens up wider angles for the receiver, as well as leaving him a bigger gap for his down-the-line return. So whether or not the gambit pays depends on the relative effectiveness of the service and return of service. As an occasional variation it may pay to serve from a position away from the centre. As a regular routine it is unlikely to do so. There are two reasons: the nearer you are to the centre of the baseline when serving, the shorter the distance the ball has to travel; by using slice you can swerve the ball in its flight far more than the receiver. Consequently you can move him around

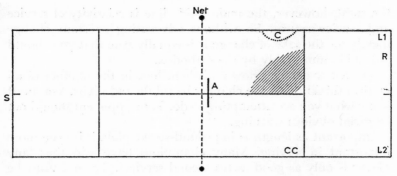

Figure 5.2

S is serving without great power and most of the time the ball is falling in the shaded area of the court. R is able to move in on the ball, run in with minimum change of direction and reach the net in a superior position along line A.

S begins serving to the arc C, forcing R to move right away from the centre of the court. Though he may hit a strong return, he must now run very fast to reach A.

This gives S a triple chance: a 'wrong footing' passing shot back to C, a cross-court pass to CC or a lob to L1 or L2.

This system works almost as well in the backhand court if S serves in the area CC.

relatively more than he can you. Certainly you have this advantage regardless of your serving position, but by swerving the service you can move him out of court while remaining yourself in the optimum court-covering position.

This advantage is not quite so marked in the left court, because the natural swerve of the ball takes it from right to left and so pulls the receiver either into court if you aim for his backhand, or to the middle of the court if you aim for the centre line of the service courts. In fact, an American twist service kicks the ball from left to right though not so sharply as a slice from right to left in the right court. In addition, though the majority of top-line players, men and women, are steadier and more accurate on the backhand than the forehand, the return is seldom as fast and is also more often predictable in direction.

There is, therefore, more chance of gain by varying your service position in the left court than there is in the right. As in the right, however, the main guide line is relativity of service and service return. So without advocating constant change merely for the sake of change it is equally true that you should not abide immutably by the orthodox.

Try a few changes now and then, but, in the manner of all tactical thinking, let the changes be subtle and slight. You must know what you are attempting to do. Your opponent should not be given obvious warning.

Important as length is in ground-stroke play, it is even more important in serving. Many champions have said that 'any player is only as good as his second service'. To that must be added: 'and the normal second service is only as good as its length'. Since your service is the shot your opponent cannot volley, it should be clear that if you serve always within an inch or two of the service line, your opponent will find it much more difficult to attack you than when you pitch the ball only half-way up the service court.

Aiming your second service near the line involves risk of double faulting, and double faulting carries a psychological penalty as well as the loss of the point. It is something which any novice reporter can count, and, without question, the number of double faults served in any match is the most widely reported statistic in the game, with aces second.

Such reporting is damaging to the morale of all but the most resilient players, for even they will seldom realise, say, that although they served 12 double faults, they won 20 points they would otherwise have lost if the services had been short instead of long, so showing a net profit of 8 points. This hypothetical count, of course, does not take into account the relative importance of the points won and lost.

So you must work out your own profit and loss accounts. To be practical, when serving in practice or against inferior opponents, aim your second service within a few inches of the service line. After a while you should find that, say, a foot seems an immense safety margin when you play a match where the fight is too tight to risk losing points by double faulting.

As in all training, second service practice should 'hurt' even more than match play.

Tony Trabert accepted the risks involved in full length

second services in 1955 when he won Wimbledon and ranked first in the world. Rod Laver did not become champion of the world until he developed a strong second service, particularly with respect to its length.

Placement depends on what you are trying to achieve. Is it to force a weak return from a poor shot, to manoeuvre your opponent into a disadvantageous court position, to put the ball beyond his reach, to bluff him by feeding his good shot so that you can hammer his weak one on key points, to get him into set routines so that he can be discomfited later?

There is never any need to hurry your service, so take your time, think about where to put the ball and why; having decided, get on your toes mentally for his return and then serve with deliberation. Take care not to be thinking when or just after you hit the ball. Once placement is decided the serve must be automatic and the mind keyed up for the return to come. All too often a thinking mind results in leaden feet.

In general, play the percentages at love–all, 15/30, 30/15, 30/30, 30/40 and 40/30. If you want to have a go, take 15/0 and 40/15 as suitable moments. Not every time, however, for your opponent will soon tumble to your habits. So occasionally you must gamble on other points.

I recall being 2–5, 0/40 down to George Godsell in the Lowther semi-finals some years ago. I served a fault and he moved to the alley in readiness to murder my second delivery. There was a wide gap on his forehand; instinct or experience told me that if I could ace him with my second ball, he would be so unnerved that he would also miss the next two returns and I would be at deuce. I felt strangely confident, went for and got the middle line ace and he made four errors on his next six strokes. The gamble won three points, not one; I took the game and then the set 7–5 and, later, the final. Afterwards, Godsell confessed how that second service ace had shattered his morale.

There can be no hard and fast rules about gambling. Timing comes through experience, but nothing develops experience so quickly or surely as continuous thought.

Perhaps the finest example of disciplined placing came from Ashley Cooper when he beat Neale Fraser in the 1958 Wimbledon final. Fraser is left-handed and his backhand typical of all southpaws. Cooper determined that every Fraser backhand return of service would have to be a backhand passing shot. Cooper served on 156 points. On 147 of them Fraser was forced to take the ball backhanded. Cooper won the final 3–6, 6–3, 6–4, 13–11, ample satisfaction for the defeat inflicted on him by Lew Hoad in the 1957 final. Despite all your skill and knowledge, you will sometimes drop service games. There is one cardinal rule to observe at such moments. Forget disappointment, anger, annoyance over real or imagined umpiring or lining errors and concentrate every scrap of your skill on breaking back in the very next game. Your opponent may relax fractionally to help you in this. Certainly you will feel more confidence at again being on level terms while he will feel a little frustration at so quickly losing an advantage so recently acquired.

Equally with service, return of service should rank as a major priority in the equipment of any ambitious player. If your service is perfect you can never lose. On the other hand, if your return of service is non-existent, you can never win.

There are two main theories about return of service. One is that one should hit savagely at all services – 'go for broke' is the popular phrase – hoping that some time four out of six or less will go in court and so bring about the break needed for the set. The other is that the ball should be returned at all costs, no matter how weakly, in the hope that the opponent's following shot will be easier to handle than his service. In match play an experienced, successful competitor will usually move up and down between these two ways of dealing with the matter.

Your basic philosophy should be adjusted to your temperament and physical attributes. If you are tall and heavily built, like Dick Savitt, you will be forced into leaning towards the 'go for broke' opinion. Receiving service, you have to cover only one quarter of the court, roughly speaking. Once you have returned the ball your opponent has that quarter and the other three as well as the target area for his placement. So unless your 'get it back anyway' return is a fairly good one, the chances are that you will not be sufficiently agile to recover balance and then run down the ensuing volley or groundstroke.

If, on the other hand, your reflexes and hand, eye and feet co-ordination work with extreme rapidity, like those of Ken

Service and Return of Service

Rosewall or Rod Laver, you are not forced to 'go for broke' against even the strongest serve–volley opponents. In fact, these two champions move and think so rapidly that they return service with power comparable with the 'go for broke' brigade.

Tony Roche also returns service very surely. Basically he aims to get the ball into play but he takes service on the rise and has such a good eye that he can dink the ball back low and at angles which stretch incoming volleyers to their limit. Receiving service, Roche probably makes more passing shots off the server's first volley than any other man in tennis. Lest any statisticians have actually logged Roche let me emphasise that that was a purely subjective judgment. Possibly Pancho Gonzales would agree. Now over forty years old, remember, he hates the continuous stretching and bending imposed on him by Roche's 'dinks'. Thus it seems the perfect theory but there are many ways of killing a cat.

Arthur Ashe ended Gonzales' amazing run in the 1969 Wimbledon singles by 'going for broke' when Gonzales served, reasoning that so tired a middle-aged man would be too stiff to move rapidly and would thus be embarrassed more by speedy returns than by softer, angled ones. 'The difference was just one step in each shot. If he were one step quicker it might have been different but if you cannot get to the ball you cannot hit it,' Ashe explained. True, the angled returns would make him bend and stretch but at least he would have sufficient time to make the moves. On the day Ashe's system worked splendidly and he seriously disrupted Gonzales' confidence as well as winning.

Gonzales is 6 ft. 3 in. tall but he moves with the ease and grace of a leopard so he is well to the 'get it back anyway' side of the fence. There is one slight disadvantage of this system and that is the way it gives the server continuous practice in other shots. He may miss a few, set you up with sitters on a few more, and seldom make a killing with the balance, but at least he experiences the continuous feel of ball on racket. This helps him in the games when he is receiving.

Vladimir Zednik, the dynamic Czech, is the same height as Gonzales but not nearly so agile. He serves with such power that on his day he is virtually unbreakable. When Czechoslovakia won the King's Cup in December 1969 he dropped service only

six times in the sixty-one he served. So he is an advocate of
'going for broke' and during this particular series it paid him a
rich dividend. In game after game all four of his returns would
crash into the net, zoom yards beyond the lines or flash past the
incoming volley without being touched. Therefore, when he did
get a few back, the incoming server frequently erred on the
volley simply through lack of feel; he had not had any volley
practice for 20 minutes or so and was out of touch in consequence.

The system you adopt inevitably relates itself to the strengths
of the server. If his service is moderate but his volleys devastating you are forced to take more risks returning than when playing a big man with a mighty service but no certainty at all in
his body balance or on the volley. Most good players return
service with greater certainty on the backhand than on the forehand. On the latter the body is in the way of the follow-
through. On the backhand the racket clears from the body after
impact and so it is simpler to obtain and maintain consistency
and direction, if not power.

The actual technique of the server can help your return of
service, or at least its effectiveness. For example, some players
fall away to their backhand side–Virginia Wade is one–so that
they are relatively slow and vulnerable to returns wide to their
forehands. Conversely, others tumble slightly towards the forehand. Here the obvious return is an angle to the backhand.

The tendency can be spotted during the early stages of a
meeting but why waste time? It will show up just as well in the
previous round, so go and have a look from the end of the court.

Many, if not most, men are more comfortable volleying shots
from the backhand than from the forehand so it may well be
you will have to add power to your backhand. This is best
achieved by moving into the ball on impact, adding thrust to
your shot and also giving you a slight forward movement which
overcomes body inertia. This should enable you to start moving
for your volley the moment your opponent strikes the ball.

There are two important factors involved here. The first is to
act on the assumption that your return is going to clear the net
and make him volley. The second is to watch the ball very carefully. What passes for good anticipation is often purely the

fruits of watching the ball carefully and so picking up direction
a yard earlier in the ball's flight from the opponent's racket.

The relative merits of down-the-line and cross-court returns
of service are analysed closely in figure 5.3. As a rough guide,

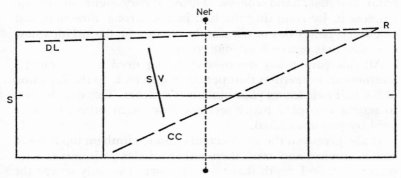

Figure 5.3

S is the serving position, R the receiver returning a slice to his
forehand and SV the position S reaches after running in and
his reach. DL represents a down-the-line return and CC one
across the court.

The advantage of DL is that the ball travels a shorter distance. The disadvantages are that the net is about five inches
higher at the sidelines than in the middle so that the ball must
travel higher. Should the server reach the return of service, he
can hit the ball at a very acute angle across the court into a
tremendous gap and the ball will be travelling away from the
receiver.

Returning the ball across court makes it travel a greater
distance but it crosses the net at its lowest point. The server's
volley to the backhand corner will not be travelling at such a
severe angle away from the receiver but a wrong footing cross-
court volley to the forehand is a good alternative for the server.

On balance, the cross-court return is better, especially if the
server is a little slow running in. The closer he gets to the net,
the more he narrows the cross-court angle but the down-the-
line gap is roughly constant so it will probably be advantageous
to use more down-the-line returns.

Against men who run in fast, throw in some return of service lobs. They are difficult to achieve accurately but their
effectiveness justifies a major effort in practice.

use more cross-court returns against a man who runs in slowly and step up the number of down-the-line returns against a man who gets in fast.

The other sure guide line is the relative strengths of his forehand and backhand volleys. Throw theory right out of the window if, by returning the ball in the 'wrong' direction, you win seven points out of ten simply because he has no idea how to volley that return into your court.

All this emphasises the overwhelming need for the mental alertness and eagerness that permit you to pick up the direction of the ball as it leaves your opponent's racket. This enables you to return into play many services that might otherwise have sped by you untouched.

It also gives you the split-second extra to climb on top of weak second services and crash them either for clean winners or with such power and depth that your opponent can only scrape the ball back as an even softer offering for you to kill.

Treat weak second services boldly and mercilessly. There is nothing more morale-destroying than finding every time you serve a fault that you are promptly crushed back on your heels by a thunderous drive which your opponent follows up to the net. Nine times out of ten your service becomes worse instead of better and what began the match as a weakness ends as a disaster. The tenth player will remain calm and probably slow down his first services to a speed which enables him to put his first service in play on most points. This move will free you from the risk of being aced and will drive you back where you cannot force the pace with your return of service. However, as realisation of the situation develops you will be able to attack his first services almost as strongly as once you hammered his second.

On the whole, in these situations the cross-court slam is geometrically the safer course. The court is four and a half feet longer diagonally than down the line and the net is six inches lower in the middle than it is at the posts. So speed is safer across court than down the line. But down-the-line shots must be used, both to exploit your opponent's backhand and to keep him guessing.

Your pattern of choice will in some ways be governed by your technique. If you produce most of your forehands from a closed

stance – that is, with the left foot in front of or across the right –
you will normally need to move considerably to arrive in a
down-the-line position in the right court. Mental laziness, lack
of confidence and the speed of your opponent's service can all
inhibit the movement and so result in a high proportion of
cross-court returns. An open stance will give you greater
flexibility and help you to hit more down-the-line returns.

In the left court the closed stance will tend to lead to returns
which go to your opponent's forehand while the open stance
will enable you to direct forehand returns in a reverse angle –
that is, from your backhand corner to his backhand. There is
one important rule to follow: be positive. If you are going to
attack a weak second service, attack it hard. Any timidity or
hesitancy will leave you languishing in the no man's land of
half-court. Remember, too, that deception can be valuable. If
you can convince your opponent during the early part of a
match that your favourite return is, say, down-the-line, you
will be increasing the chances of your cross-court return scoring
vital points in the closing stages.

This is, perhaps, more effective in doubles than in singles. I
used to make it a habit to go for the net man's sideline at least
once in every early game and then, later, having ceased for
most of a set, to return to the down-the-line shot in the final
stages.

The dangers of this return are less great than they appear:
you know in advance what you are going to do while the man
at the net does not, so your chances of reaching his volley are
strong. The other useful feature is that such returns will, early
on, tend to inhibit him from poaching and so free you from the
worry of the net man's dashing across and knocking your
orthodox returns for volley winners.

The important thing about service return is to watch the ball,
forgetting everything else but where the lines are. They are
constant. They do not move around. Once you have become
accustomed to where they are from every spot on your side of
the net – when your knowledge of court geometry is complete –
you are equipped to return every ball to some predetermined
place on either sideline on the opponent's side of the net. On no
account should you attempt to keep half an eye on him so as to

outsmart him. Ignore the opponent. He is moving and a moving target is much more difficult than that sitting one, a fixed line.

So, watch the ball, ignore your opponent and concentrate on returning the ball near a side line. If it is a strong service, tend to go for the line nearer to his weaker wing; you should have discovered which this is during pre-match study and confirmed it during the knock-up and the early stages of the match. If the service is not so strong you need not be quite so stereotyped and can vary your returns with severer drives to his stronger wing's sideline.

Do not hesitate about feeding him a few returns to his strengths in order to build up his complacency. Complacency is the arch enemy of alertness and the last thing you want in a crisis is an alert opponent.

What action should you take before you actually start to return service? You lose the toss and your opponent decides to serve. You elect to play one game in the sun because that has always been your custom. Why?

If you win the set 6–1 you play four games with your back to the sun and three looking in to it. But if you are that much superior to him, how much does that one game extra with your back to the sun matter? A 6–2 set means you play four games in the sun and four with your back to it. A 6–3 set means you are not all that superior to your opponent so you need to seize any advantages you can. Yet by starting with one in the sun, you actually play five games looking into it and only four away from it. You needed help, and you gave it to your opponent instead. How stupid. Thereafter, the set has to be an even number of games so you will play an equal number of games in the sun and shade.

So the critical match is the one you win 6–3, 3–6, 6–3, 3–6, 6–3. The choice is yours, but by losing the toss and taking one in the shade instead of the sun you give yourself an advantage in the first, third and fifth sets. Thus in both best of three and best of five set matches you have a slight advantage in the final sets. If you win the first set 6–3 and lose the second 4–6 it is true that you start the third set in the sun and so suffer a slight disadvantage.

The permutations are many and it is up to each player to

decide his own policy. Since I believe that winning the first set is preferable to losing it, my preference is for playing the first game not looking into the sun.

Mike Sangster went even further than this, for even when he won the toss, he normally chose to play the first game in the shade. He had an additional reason, for he reckoned that powerful servers need a game or two to loosen up. Thus he argued that the server's stiffness plus the sun in his eyes would assist in an immediate break-through of service. Naturally he had taken great care to free his own muscles from stiffness so that when he served in the second game all he needed to overcome was the sun in his eyes. It proved a successful system for Sangster.

As in all phases of tennis, return of service is a battle of wits—yours against his. No matter how thoroughly you understand the theories put forward in this chapter, it is their application which tells in the end.

Go out on court and think. Learn to be physically involved to the limit, mentally engaged to the last degree yet still sufficiently detached to take an outsider's view of the match as a whole. When you can do this you will be on your way to mastering the second most vital factor in competitive tennis.

6 · Defence Against Net Play

You may hold your service games nine times out of ten and return service 80 per cent of the time. Yet in modern tennis, especially men's singles, this is not enough. Unless your returns are very strong, you will be forced by a volley to make at least one more shot in the rally and as your opponent will be camped on or near the net, that shot must be a good one.

Thus defence against net play is another vital aspect of success. Its first rule is never panic. Do not give your opponent an easy victory through a series of mistakes due to fright. Force him to win every point with a volleyed placement you cannot reach and return. The Deloford v. Roberts match discussed in Chapter four (p. 53) provides a dramatic example of how panic measures make life easy for the volleyer. Remember, Deloford made only two volleys, both losers, and yet won the match by net rushing. Never let that happen to you. I repeat, with emphasis, never panic.

This rule applies particularly when the match is nearly at its end for it is then that net rushers tend to gain their greatest rewards.

The second secret of successful defence against net rushers is to watch the ball, forget the opponent and learn always to know – to feel within you – exactly where the lines are and, remember, they do not move. By trying to keep half an eye on the opponent you may occasionally out-guess him by spotting a movement and so firing your shot in the appropriate direction. But this distraction from the ball costs a lot of points through unnecessary mistakes, so do not fall for it.

Rather, keep your eye on the ball, remember your court geometry and out-think him. You will not always do so but by concentrating on the ball you will hit very much better shots so that even when he does volley them, the chances of your reaching the ball and having another attempt at passing him will be greatly magnified.

The third secret is use of top spin, that is, spin which rotates the top of the ball forwards, and so increases its wind resistance relative to the bottom of the ball, causing the ball to dip in flight. When your opponent is 26 yards away on the opposite baseline, the loss of land speed relative to a flat drive is important. But the main loss is over the full length of the court. At the half-way distance, at the net, the loss of speed relative to the land is slight and more than offset by the difficulties the sudden dip causes to the volleyer.

In normal ground-stroke rallies it is advantageous and wise to make your strokes when the ball has just passed the top point in its bounce. Whenever you sense or see your opponent running to the net, move in and take the ball on the rise. Remember that if you can play the ball effectively a yard farther forward, you will be gaining two yards–the yard of flight to you and from you. This should correspond to one running pace by your opponent, leaving him five or six feet farther back from the net than he would have been had you taken the ball just after the top of its bounce.

Figure 6.1 shows the effect.

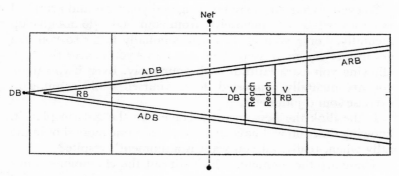

Figure 6.1

The amount of court left open by a volleyer with a 12-feet stretch against a man who lets the ball drop (DB) and one who takes it on the rise (RB). Against DB he reaches the position VDB. The lines ADB show how much court is open. Against RB he only reaches position VRB. The lines ARB show that more court is open for a passing shot.

Defence Against Net Play

Changing from a falling ball to a rising ball demands an alert mind, to realise that you are to be attacked from the net, and an adaptable stroke technique. Any deficiencies in either factor will tend to increase your mistakes and so cancel out your gain in effectiveness from hitting the ball while it is still rising.

Judgment and freedom from fear are vital. Judgment is needed in deciding whether to attempt a direct passing shot, to lob or to use a 'dink' in an effort to force a weakish volley that will simplify a passing shot next time. When you choose the first, natural optimism makes you believe—or hope—that you are about to make a point-winning stroke. You know when making a dink—that is, a softish, dropping angled return—that he will reach it and the rally will continue. It is easy to accept this at the start of matches and when you are physically and mentally fresh.

At four games all in the final set when you are hot, tiring and perhaps not a little anxious, instinct tells you to hit the ball hard. This is especially true if you are being hurried and hurt. These are the times when mental detachment is vital. Maybe it is right to give way to instinct and hit the ball as hard as you can. Eight times out of ten it will be wrong.

So even if your lungs are bursting and your legs and arms feel as if they will detach themselves from your body, do not give up mentally. Force yourself to run fractionally faster so you can get in just one more step. This will move you nearer the ball, allowing you extra latitude with your reply. Even if you think you are mentally exhausted, force yourself while running to exercise sound judgment.

Is the dink the best answer? Have you the guts to play it, knowing that you will have to chase at least one more shot in the rally when, really, all you want is a moment's respite?

These are the moments which sift out the champions. They do not try an odds-against slam just to win or lose the point immediately and so end the physical and mental torture. They never give up. They use their judgment. It may sometimes be a wrong judgment but, mentally, they are accepting the pressures and staying with their opponent. And, if you stay with your opponent long enough, your willpower must prevail and victory will be yours.

80

Defence Against Net Play

Of the men dominating international tennis in the early 1970s, Tony Roche and John Newcombe are the best exponents of dinking while Arthur Ashe and Rod Laver are best when it comes to outright passing shots. The corollary of the dink is the lob: as the former tempts the volleyer to run in even faster in order to close right in on the net, the latter forces him to hold back. And whenever he is in two minds he is vulnerable to a fast passing shot hit down the line or across the court.

Ability to dispense a baffling mixture of dinks, lobs and straight passes depends on sound, controlled ground strokes. Even when you have developed these, there will be days when your opponents still swamp you with their agility and finality on the volley. Then you will have to decide whether it is best to go on hitting good ground strokes which he is volleying for winners in the hope he will eventually crack, or to try to race him to the net even though you are only moderately skilled at volleying; there is always the chance that his ground strokes are worse than your volleys. If this is the case and you can consistently race him to the net, the percentages change to your favour.

Such tactics were used to perfection by René Lacoste in the semi-finals of the 1926 American Championships. He wrote:[1]

'I owed the beating of Cochet to tactics entirely new to me. During the first two sets, playing from the back of the court in accordance with my custom, I was constantly dominated. At the beginning of the third set, risking all for all, I attacked by coming constantly to the net. I did not play particularly well at the net on that day. If I conducted all my matches as I played the end of this one I should not win often, but experience proved that it was better for me to play badly at the net, to oblige Cochet to play worse at the back of the court, than to play well at the back of the court and allow him to play better at the net.'

Lacoste went on to beat Jean Borotra in the final and so capture the title for France for the first time.

Rod Laver, too, used roughly the same approach while recovering from a two sets to love deficit to beat Roy Emerson in the final of the 1962 French Championship, though this is a simplification of the event.

[1] *Lacoste on Tennis* by René Lacoste.

Defence Against Net Play

The times to go for a passing shot down the line and across the court have already been discussed in Chapter five (p. 73). They should be studied again in the context of this chapter. Similarly, the theory and practice of lobbing is covered in Chapter three (p. 42). Again, these pages should be read in connection with the present chapter.

You may still be unable to pass your opponent. Angela Buxton met this difficulty against Ann Shilcock in match after match during the 1950s. No matter which side she aimed, Miss Shilcock always seemed to be there. Then came the 1956 final of the British Covered Court Championships. The wooden court gives every possible aid to a volleyer and the prospect was gloomy. Instead of trying carefully to place the ball, Miss Buxton moved towards it when Miss Shilcock attacked from the net. Then she hit it hard without much regard for direction—sometimes even straight at Miss Shilcock. The change of defensive tempo worked like a charm, as the record books tell at a glance.

You can and should begin your defence against net attacks before your opponent actually reaches the net. When he is serving this is scarcely possible. When you are serving it is. For example, your service is not strong enough to force him back to the baseline. Instead, he is moving forward every time, taking the ball on the rise and running in behind his returns. In such a situation, every time you serve down the middle you are permitting him to reach the net in the best possible position. Accept, therefore, that he will be following in and serve wide to the sidelines even if you are feeding his best shot, which may be his forehand. Though he will return the ball strongly, he will be forced to race for the centre of his court.

This leaves you with three possibilities: a wrong footing shot back to the spot from which he returned service; an angled return to the opposite sideline; a lob, preferably to the corner he is racing away from (see figure 5.2, p. 67).

All this demonstrates the variety of methods open to a baseliner in opposing a net rusher. You may introduce some psychological cunning into your defence. Perhaps you will be able to con the volleyer into believing that your favourite passing shot is across court by feeding him a great number, switching only to your best, down-the-line passes when you specially need a point. Then, having got the point, returning to the non-favourite pass until another crisis arises, as it surely will.

Defensive skill is essential. A defensive mental attitude is a severe handicap. Experiment and be bold. Never allow yourself to be hustled into a state of panic. Get on the ball quickly and do not give away cheap points. Make him work hard for his games. When you have fully developed this attitude and these techniques you will be a danger to everyone.

7 · Tactics that Win Against the Odds

To those involved deeply in the highest levels of championship play, it is now generally accepted that success derives 25 per cent from technique and 75 per cent from mental and physical attributes.

Those mental attributes are especially vital in planning and maintaining tactical schemes when actually on court. This can scarcely be over-emphasised, for time and again one sees players, even of the highest class, competing in a state of 'waking sleep'. They will lose point after point through exactly the same sequence of shots without having the slightest idea of what is happening. The Rod Lavers of tennis grow fat on such shortcomings, which are common to many players.

Seven years separate the following extracts, which are from recordings he made for me. The first followed his win over Roy Emerson in the Final of the 1962 French Singles Championship, after Emerson had taken the first two sets.

'When you are nearly beaten it is no good waiting for the other fellow to make a mistake,' he said. 'You might as well have a go and force him to do something. I closed right in to the net for my second volleys. Emerson doesn't lob much and so I chanced it.'

In 1969, after he had beaten Arthur Ashe in the Wimbledon semi-finals I said to him, 'You'll be in trouble if Ashe ever learns the lob.'

'But he doesn't,' Laver replied simply, so revealing why he had again camped right on top of the net as part of his attack, although this had given Ashe the first set.

So Laver's knowledge of two players' habits of play enabled him to survive crises which might well have ended his grand slam activities in 1962 and 1969. His sharp knowledge of John Newcombe came to his aid in the 1969 Wimbledon final, as this recording reveals with great clarity:

'But the tension was no greater than in my previous finals. Each time one walks on the centre court the sensation is the same. I knew John would not yield very easily, and that turned out to be the case, but I felt quite confident.

'Taking the match as a whole, it seemed I was more consistent than in the matches against Stan Smith and Arthur Ashe. My return of service was surer and I volleyed and played generally a more consistent type of game.

'From my end of the court John appeared to be in good form. He plays softer and more cleverly than most realise. His shots are flat and their direction disguised deceptively. He forces you to hit low volleys all the time and unless you have good timing and touch it is tough to put the ball out of his reach.

'When you do not he throws up those high lobs which put him right back in the rallies. He disguised his game and was penetrating at times though not as strongly as I expected. He used his forehand more often than I expected instead of running round the ball. I had hoped he would and so leave me with two different plays on serve; as well as going down the centre I would also be able to push the ball wide.

'After the first set John became very tough. He lobbed a lot, not that that normally worries me, but his were so high and so deep and I had to wait so long for them to come down that it was really difficult to smash them continually without making errors.

'He was lobbing within a yard or so of the baseline all the time, I missed a couple of smashes just barely and that cost me a couple of my service games.

'He was also mixing his game cleverly, dinking the ball astutely and disguising his little angled shots deceptively. I wasn't getting any fresher and when he took a 4–1 lead in the third set it did not look too good. When you face the fact of being two sets to one down and are fairly tired there is always a lot to be concerned about. You grow tired when you are continually going backwards and forwards for smashes off deep lobs. But my tiredness was mainly through being puffed. My legs felt strong but needing a little more rest so I slowed the game down to my standard between the rallies. John was pretty slow himself but I still slowed my own game and allowed him to wait; that allowed me to get my breath back.

'You find yourself thinking more clearly in a position like that than when you are winning easily. You have to concentrate more and to make a determined, concentrated effort for six or more games to fight back into the match. I think my best tennis of the entire final came when I was 1–4 down in the third set.

'When I went on court I knew I had to keep the ball low so I intended hitting over the ball to keep him under pressure. If I could keep the ball dipping below the level of the net when he came in to volley it meant I would be able to get a good crack at the second passing shot. This was where I felt I could capitalise if he did not serve as well as he actually did much of the time.

'There was not a lot more I could have done at that stage. I was going for shots and in the end they clicked. Like me, he was pushing for depth on service and he ended the game which gave me the break for 3–4 by double faulting. That was a good game for me because I reached love–thirty with a chancy sort of sharply angled backhand volley which came off and gave me the better of the play. That was the game which changed the whole final.

'What pleased me most about the closing stages was my service. It was consistent, I backed it up well and I wasn't broken. But I felt I was in some danger in that third set.

'It was a tough match, probably the hardest of any of my finals at Wimbledon.

'John was able to keep the ball in play a lot more than my other opponents and when you are under pressure all the time with the atmosphere of finals day it is a nervous strain trying to keep control all the time.'

In the 1950s I was personally involved as tactical adviser in a number of matches in which men and women were successful in beating opponents who had hitherto always defeated them with great ease. Some of these successes I explained in an article which bears repetition.

'Quite the most neglected aspect of coaching is in tactics. Many people do not believe it is possible–even wise–to teach youngsters to think lest the very act of thinking inhibits the power and freedom of their hitting. The few who do believe in the value of the correct shot, or sequence of shots, at the right moment mostly either fail to be bold enough in their thinking or lack the necessary experience to advise on this all important facet of match winning.

'There is also the natural reluctance of 99 players out of every 100 to apply their full powers of concentration to the tasks of using their own strengths to exploit their opponents' weaknesses or tendencies, whilst simultaneously protecting their own weaknesses from damaging attack.

'To emphasise that judicious study and thinking can produce large swings between players whose techniques remained unchanged I shall draw on a number of examples with which I have been associated.

'The first concerns Sven Davidsson, who had just previously lost to Beppy Merlo, and who had to meet him in the semi-finals of the French Championships of 1956.

'At that stage in his career, Davidsson had a marked preference for going to the net behind deep drives to the backhand. But this approach gave Merlo the finest possible chance to exploit his double-handed swat; clearly, it could not be used.

Merlo's weakness

'Observation of Merlo's quarter-final victory over Seixas had revealed his marked preference for hitting his forehand passing shot down the line, a preference which became a necessity when an angled shot to his double-handed side preceded an approach to the net behind a deep backhand drive down the forehand line. Such tactics were well within the abilities of Davidsson's technique, so they were recommended and adopted. Of thirteen critical points played to this plan Davidsson won eleven, a ratio more than sufficient to avenge the recent defeat and give him a straight set win.

'The next concerns Angela Buxton who lost in straight sets to Darlene Hard in the 1956 Sutton final and then had to meet her in the Queen's final a few weeks later.

'Clearly, Miss Hard was not going to be kept away from the net and her volleying and covering ability against orthodox play had been amply demonstrated at Sutton.

Tactics that Win Against the Odds

'It was necessary, therefore to ensure that she reached the net in the worst positions possible. This was achieved by sacrificing deep drives for shorter angled ones aimed at the junctions of the side and service lines.

'Thus, most of her approaches began from outside the alley, leaving the maximum chance to outplace, wrong foot, or lob her. Again, a straight set loss was converted to a straight set win.

'Miss Buxton also used a preconceived plan worked out from observation to turn a series of 6–3, 6–3 or worse defeats by Patricia Ward into the first of a series of straight set wins.

'Miss Ward, a beautifully fluent stroke maker of above-average playing intelligence, was finally observed to be slow on the turn. A campaign of fast, moderately well placed drives from side to side with the fourth or fifth back to the same spot proved the match winning gambit.

'Till this year's Hard Court Championships Christine Truman had never won more than two games in a set from Ann Shilcock, and that included the Covered Court Championship final which had been played one month earlier.

Unthinking policy

'Miss Truman's natural, automatic, unthinking policy is a bang to the forehand, followed by a bang to the backhand and up to the net. This in no way embarrasses Miss Shilcock who, in their earlier meetings, had coped with sufficient time to spare to intersperse many long loopy drives–drop shot gambits with her normal net game.

'However, Miss Shilcock's forehand drive takes her a long time to execute mentally and is therefore at its best when she can execute it at the end of a smooth, unruffled run. Her other shots are affected considerably by the day to day functioning of her forehand. At the net she is very quick.

'This led to the formulation of this three-point tactical plan for Miss Truman.

    (a) To direct her driving so that Miss Shilcock was forced to play as many ground strokes as possible on the turn, but with special emphasis on the forehand.

    (b) To repel the net attack with a barrage of lobs played

      off her initial approach shot and not when forced to do
      so by a severe volley.

  (c) To counter possible drop shots by moving forward a
      step after making each shot, thus to be in a mental and
      mobile state to move up court quickly.

'Sound execution of the plan enabled Miss Truman to reach match point for a simple straight set victory and eventually to win in three sets.

'Plans do not always work; but they are still useful, especially in team play.

'After watching Merlo at Bournemouth this year it seemed Michael Davies could beat him through sheer stamina plus back court shots, steadily aimed to reduce the angles offered to Merlo for placements.

'In play, however, it turned out that Davies, who takes a rising ball when attacking or playing with a mentally offensive attitude, hits a dropping ball when he is out to defend. So Merlo was able to run Davies twice as far as he ran himself and, ultimately, he left the court the winner and the fresher man.

'Later that afternoon Bill Knight discussed possible ways of beating Merlo, including a repeat of the Davies plan. Since Knight is neither so mobile nor so sure off the ground as Davies, it was only too apparent that in such methods lay sure defeat. Consequently, come what may, Knight had to attack as much as he could.

'However, the Davies match had shown that Merlo was somewhat vulnerable to changes of pace, length and spin, and that he did not do much with heavily cut balls short down the middle of the court.

'Using the latter to protect himself from Merlo's cunning placements, bumping heavily topped drives to Merlo's backhand corner and varying his service as much as possible, Knight achieved a win which is now history.

'A somewhat more complex plan enabled Gerald Oakley to beat Geoffrey Paish some years ago at Bournemouth when Paish was at his best. Paish had–still has–a remarkably quick eye and was well able to cope with pace. He also possessed a fine drop shot and the all-round control to move a steady opponent around the court, though he was sometimes a trifle slow to bring this into operation. He was also a shade vulnerable to changes of pace.

'Thus, the plan was to soft ball Paish for one set and then, whichever way it went, to switch suddenly and immediately to the attack. When serving, to concentrate on a deep, high kicking delivery to his backhand which was to be followed in.

'The soft balling won a 9–7 first set and the sudden switch to attack completed the discomfiture and won the match.

Technical skill a necessity

'All these tactical plans necessitated a high degree of technical ability but the players concerned all possessed this. In the first five cases correct channelling of the technical ability enabled them to convert earlier loss or losses into victory; in some cases the swing by score was spectacular.

'The tactics, however, could only be planned because a good deal of detailed information about the opponent was available.

'For that reason I strongly recommend every ambitious player to keep a note book or card index system in which is recorded every possible piece of information about contemporary players. This should not only be the observations of the player himself or herself. Discussions with other players while watching will bring out a lot of ideas which otherwise would have lain dormant.

'As well as keeping the notebook, time should be spent on court playing shots and thinking sequentially. Most players think only of where they will hit the immediate shot but, just as a champion billiards player is always playing to build position, so a tennis player can manoeuvre for a coup three or four shots ahead.

'Much of the time it is not necessary in theory. One's technical ability is either so superior or inferior that the result is a foregone conclusion. However, the things practised today and tomorrow take a year or more to become effective, so even when winning–or losing–easily it pays to think.'

Different players vary in their assessment of the most important points in each game other than the game points themselves.

Tactics that Win Against the Odds

Many like to win the first point so as to take an immediate lead. Others become angry if they reach thirty–love and then lose the following point through carelessness. They like to climb on top and hammer their opponents into the ground.

What is your preference, to play when you are ahead or when you are trailing? Contrary to popular opinion, it is far easier to play well when behind than when in the lead. Take the case of the 5–2 lead or deficit.

First the deficit. If you are 2–5 down you will (a) normally feel the set has slipped away and (b) decide to make a last, strong effort to save it. Because of (a) you will probably be released from nervous tension – the set has gone, so what? – and this will banish some of the inhibitions which have been restricting your earlier efforts.

Thus the determination to fight back will be accompanied by the best kind of mental attitude.

The danger will arise if and when you reach five all. Subconsciously you are then likely to feel you are already home, or nearly so, and thus ease your pressure. Simultaneously, the relaxation you felt when almost beaten at 2–5 will now be replaced by the tension which caused all the problems that put you behind in the first place.

Meanwhile, how about the man over the net with the 5–2 lead? There is a common tendency to choke at this stage, mentally, physically or both.

Mentally, there are many players who either become too cautious or too bold. In the first case they reduce slightly the pressure which has gained the lead. In the second they become too eager, try to exceed their optimum hitting speed and fall into error. Either of these faults when coinciding with a major effort from the man behind can make the difference of one or more points a game, a really big handicap. Certainly it is sufficient to transfer ascendancy from the leading player to the one who is behind.

What is the answer? The old adage is 'never change a winning game'. A better one in this situation is 'slightly intensify a winning game'.

If aggression has gained the lead, watch the ball even more carefully so you can hit it six inches or a foot nearer to its

91

bounce than earlier. When short returns come over, be extra alert to move in on the ball to stroke it firmly into the gap.

Avoid trying to end a rally merely because you feel it should be over by now. If you are a volleyer, close in and try for firmness rather than blinding speed. Too many people equate aggression with slashing at the ball. The deftest of drop shots is aggressive when your opponent is poised on the baseline for a crushing drive. Attack is more a mental state than anything else.

On the other hand, if defensive play has established the lead, strengthen that defence. Bear in mind that your opponent is trying harder so if the rallies grow longer avoid panicking and trying to end them at the wrong time.

Be prepared to run a little faster and a good deal farther. Remain calm when he moves up to the net. Remember that he may come in a little quicker so be prepared to lob with your first shot. Do not hit too hard in desperation or from fear.

Dictate to the ball and do not let it control you in your placements or pace. Stick to 'traffic signals' tennis.

Whether attacking or defending, make sure of getting your first shot into play—and your second—and third. Treat each ball on its merits and try to win the first point, then the second and third. Be fearful of letting him back into the game and so try even harder for the fourth point.

Stay with him. Make him work like a slave for every point and do not give him any cheap points. You will need endurance, physical and mental. But so will he. Make sure his will yield first, even if it takes many deuces to finish each game.

Be miserly on break points because you may not get many. When Rosewall beat Newcome for a £5,000 first prize at Wembley in November 1968 he had only six chances to break service in four sets and he seized five of them. In the 1970 Wimbledon final he had 18 chances to break Newcombe's service, won only three of them . . . and he lost.

When he lost to Martin Riessen in the final of the Rothmans £10,000 international tournament at London's Albert Hall in March 1970 he had seven break points, failed to win any of them and Riessen won 6–4, 6–2.

Riessens' method of 'playing the percentages' was unusual for he hit every ball with all his strength. He reasoned correctly that by playing at normal speed he would be outclassed. So, he chanced making mistakes as the only way of mastering a superior stroke maker.

It is always helpful to know how your opponent is feeling and one doesn't always have to be a psychologist to spot the signs, even though Allen Fox of the U.S.A. does have a Ph.D. in psychology. He is also in or near the top ten tennis players in his country.

He contributed an article to the July 1968 issue of *Lawn Tennis* which included these relevant passages.

'I'm not a clinical psychologist so I have not studied the workings of the human mind deeply but I've read enough and taken sufficient courses to have a certain amount of insight–possibly more than the average person–and I enjoy watching my opponent to see how he is doing and what he is thinking, and to sense when he is weakening and so on–what psychological problems he is having–but it is not a crucial thing. Generally there is nothing I can do about it except perhaps try a little harder.

'Everybody has signs which show when they are on the brink of cracking. It depends on the particular player. Some drop their heads and start to drag, their shots lose a little length, and that is the time you should crowd right on them.

'They all do it in different ways. Some of the Americans start hitting three times as hard when they are edgy and very nervous and you can sense that. If they do that, I have to adjust my game accordingly because I try to fit it into the way the match is going.

'I like to hear players start talking to themselves but it depends on the player. It often helps concentration if you talk to yourself a little. It gets sort of lonely out on the court and its fun to have something to say. I enjoy hearing a voice.

'Certain players, when they are ahead, are quick to play, quick to change sides, quick to pick up balls. When they are discouraged they drag at a snail's pace.

'What you do and when you see these things depends on your game and the opponents. There are certain serves it is good to use when the other fellow is discouraged. For instance, I find it is good to serve wide to the forehand. It is a shot the receiver has to be quick on; you have to be keen and leap out and slap it with your wrist. If you are discouraged you are going to be slow and sloppy and soft.

'Generally you attack if you feel the opponent is weakening but the main thing I try when I feel he is discouraged is to tighten up my own game. I try not to give him anything. If he is discouraged but he hits a ball in the corner I don't try a 100–1 passing shot down the line but I toss it up nice and high and let him think about an overhead.

'Make it tough for him when he is discouraged because then you can run off a lot of games in a hurry.

'Big sluggers can afford to have a more relaxed attitude.'

What is the best thing when you get 'the elbow'?

'When you get "the elbow" (nervous tension freezes your arm) you've had it. There's little you can do. You can take a few deep breaths and try to relax but if you play the point while you've still got "the elbow" you will lose it for sure–unless your opponent has got it even worse than you.

'The real secret is to get yourself into a state when you are in a semi-trance on the court. You don't think about the point or the game or what the publicity will be afterwards, who you are playing or anything. The best state to be in is where you watch the ball and hit the shot and forget about everything else. Keep thinking down to a minimum. It takes too much time and you don't have any to spare out there. You think between games and before the match but on the court it should be all reflex.

'Thinking is done in the cortex and it is a slow process compared with reflex.'

8 · Winning Tactics in Doubles

A survey carried out by *Lawn Tennis* during the 1969 Wills Open Championships at Bristol showed that the public enjoy watching men's doubles almost as much as they do men's singles.

This is understandable, for it is fast and exciting, two factors which make it great fun to play. There is also a shared responsibility, so that losing need not be quite so dampening as in singles while winning is not quite so personal in its 'you or me' effects on pride.

There is also less court space in which to hit winners; in singles you defend 117 square yards of court, in doubles only 78. Hence tactics, placement and court position are changed and, in some ways, made more important.

One major factor differentiates singles from doubles. In singles defensive methods quite frequently win. In doubles they seldom or never succeed. The power of the opponents may force you on the defensive but your object must always be to seize the initiative. In singles it is often advantageous to accept a defensive, relatively negative role.

Thus the importance of the first blow becomes immediately apparent and the first blow in any rally is the service. In singles it is always dangerous to lose a service game. Dropping service in top class doubles comes nearer to disaster. So every aspect of this particular stroke and those which immediately follow it – return of service, first volley, return of first volley – assumes immense importance.

So far as the server is concerned, he should set himself two tasks – to force a weak return and to run in fast to reach a parallel position with his partner at the net.

The reason for this should be apparent. The court is only 36 feet wide so that each man has only 18 feet to cover. His reach with racket and one step either way is of the order of 14 feet. Two steps will more than blanket the 18 feet. At the net the angles offered are wide and the time saved in hitting the ball immense. In modern doubles–men's, women's or mixed–victory goes to the stronger servers and volleyers most of the time.

Untouchable aces are spectacular and great crowd pleasers– and how one's ego is increased by the enthusiastic applause that follows a service ace. Yet how dangerous it is to pander to that applause by trying for more aces.

There is, of course, a necessity to try for an occasional ace, if only to inhibit the receiver from becoming over confident and moving in on the ball.

The major requirement is to subdue the receiver; to force him back and to keep him guessing. Faulting with the first service takes the pressure off the receiver, even if your second service carries as much power and length as your first. Very few receivers will feel the truth of this in their hearts and so every time you fault the receiver's confidence will zoom upwards. Because success is so tied to confidence, the chances of his making a strong return are improved disproportionately to the actualities of the situation.

The essence of good doubles serving, then, is consistently to put in a first ball pitched right up to the service line, in the right court down the middle line, in the left court either on the centre line or wide to the backhand. It must be of sufficient penetration to prevent the receiver moving forward when making his stroke. Therein lies the rub, for a good player–and throughout this book I have considered 'good' as someone of similar standard to yourself–will soon accustom himself to stereotyped services, whether they speed forward at 100 m.p.h. or crawl over the net at a fifth of that speed.

So the inevitable three-quarter pace serve deep down the middle line must be varied by occasional changes of spin, pace and direction. When? The temptation is to say that you should do this on unimportant points and that on key points–40/30, 30/40 etc.–you should play it safe. But that in itself is stereotyped.

No, there is no definite rule which can be postulated. Certainly never make it easy for your opponent on key points but what is making it easy? A nervous player frequently does not relish time to think so a fast service is far more to his liking than a slow spinner which gives him ample time to see you charging up to the net.

On the other hand, a medium paced spinner may suit a phlegmatic, slightly slower moving receiver because it gives him time to make his stroke.

So the essence of good tactics is to keep the other man guessing; to be one jump ahead of him in your thinking. Never overdo the variety, though, for then the variety itself becomes stereotyped. So play the orthodox percentage about 80 per cent of the time, especially on key points.

The exception is when the receiver has a marked weakness. In singles there is always a chance your opponent may find some way of defending himself. In doubles, with a man posted on the net to menace the receiver, there is little chance of this happening.

Statistics taken in championship doubles show almost a three to one ratio of points won or lost when the first serve goes in whilst on second serves there is a slight balance in favour of the receiver. Further, the chances of the server's partner at the net cutting off and killing the return of service (poaching) on the first ball are high whilst on the second they are almost non-existent.

The serving position in doubles differs from singles. In the latter the centre of the baseline bisects the angle the server has to cover. In doubles his partner is covering half the court so the server's best spot will be approximately half way along the baseline between the centre mark and the outside side line.

Since he will normally be attacking the backhand, the position in the right court will be nearer to the centre mark and in the left court a little more out towards the sideline. If you go too far right in the right court the service must travel along a course which is swinging across to the receiver's forehand. Compare lines AA, and BB, in figure 8.1. If the service from A is slow or slightly badly placed, the receiver will be able to run round the ball and take it on his forehand. From B he has a better margin of safety.

Figure 8.2 shows the converse when serving in the left court. though the advantage of moving out is less marked than moving a little nearer to the middle in the right court. Perhaps a little variation in both courts is a good idea for it will help to keep the receiver guessing.

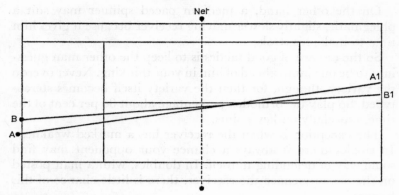

Figure 8.1

Serving to the right court.

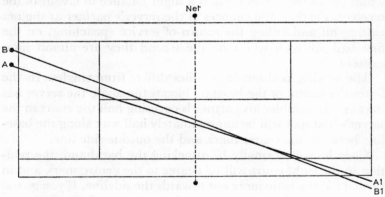

Figure 8.2

Serving to the left court.

Most top class doubles players favour the American twist service in doubles. It increases control and allows extra time to reach the net. If a cannonball flat serve does not win the point outright the server can be at a disadvantage for he will only have had time to take a couple of forward paces and the receivers may well reach the vital net position first.

Thus the service must be followed in fast—and without hesitation. Something like 80 per cent of all servers hesitate

momentarily to see if the first ball is a fault. It costs them one—
even two paces. So serve, ignore that you may fault and get in
as close as you can to the net for your first volley.

Arrange with your partner beforehand who is to cover the
lob. If he is adept at poaching, it may be preferable for you to
move in marginally less quickly so that you can change direction to chase the lobs.

If he is not a lively poacher, let him move back two or three
feet to concentrate on covering the whole of his half of the court
plus all lobs, whether they be over his own head or yours. Then
you can run in fast and often pick up the loose return, hitting the
ball with extra power gained from the momentum of your fast
forward run.

On the whole more pressure is imposed on the receiver by an
active poacher but the primary method of winning points is by
establishing the superior net position. If you or your partner are
not effective poachers settle for the net man covering the lobs
and his half of the net until such time as you both have, through
intensive high speed practice, acquired the knack of interception.

Running in fast will inevitably lead to the receivers lobbing
fairly frequently, either immediately or following the first volley.

It is commonplace for both men to retreat, much old time
teaching having demanded that partners always remain parallel.
It is also caused by the man not actually smashing the ball taking too much notice of his partner's actual stroke. This is quite
wrong.

Whenever your partner is clearly going to take the lob overhead in the air expect him to make an aggressive kill.

The average return to a powerful kill is another lob, frequently a short one. If you are parallel you have to run forward
to kill it. If you are already positioned at the net you have nothing else to do but kill the ball beyond reach of the opponents.

If instead of lobbing they drive, you are ideally placed to
poach and end the rally. So concentrate always on your 'off the
ball' court positioning, especially when your partner is hitting
aggressive smashes or volleys. Doubles is a game of attack so
crowd the net. Agree with your partner that your kills and
volleys will be placed deep down the centre of the court until

such time as a short return can be bounced diagonally over the side netting. Then your 'off the ball' position can be near to a dominant spot by the centre band of the net.

Assuming a strong service down the middle and an average return, where should the first volley be placed?

Diagram 8.3 shows dramatically how little room is offered to the receiving pair when the ball is volleyed deep to 'A'. P represents the server's partner's reach, which is slightly greater than that of S, the server who has followed in, because he is already at the net and so can leap immediately to right or left.

The broken line XX represents the shortest length a fast drive can be expected to pitch and is therefore a limiting factor of the angle open to the receivers. Top spin or dinks will move XX nearer to the net and so increase the angle.

The broken line F represents the line of the first volley and this raises a vital point when related to RP, the reach of the receiver's partner.

If the service is long, well placed and fairly powerful, RP will not be able to move farther forward than shown because the incoming server will probably be able to ram a volley straight down his throat. On the other hand, if the service is weak, RP will be able to move nearer the net because his partner will be

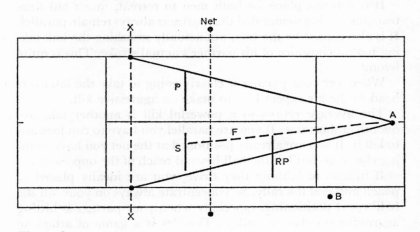

Figure 8.3

Why deep on the first volley?

able to force the ball down to the server's feet. This will limit the power of his first volley or half volley and cut off the deep first volley.

In such situations the server may decide it is preferable to aim his first volley to spot B in anticipation of RP moving across to poach any volley aimed deep down the centre. So the point has become one of guess and counter guess in which speed—of the server running in, of the receiver crowding in on the weak service, of the receiver's partner poaching—is a key factor. The faster and more daring the receiver's partner is, the more necessary it becomes to serve a first ball deep down the centre line and to get in fast. Once you and your partner are commanding the net the effectiveness of a poacher is considerably reduced. The danger lies in reaching the net.

A further study of court geometry as detailed in earlier chapters shows how angled volleys offer your opponents greater gaps and scope than those down the middle. In singles one man is defending 27 feet of baseline so there is always the chance of an angled volley evading his reach. In doubles two men are covering 18 feet each and by good covering even this figure is lessened. So simple mathematics show a minimum reduction of $33\frac{1}{3}$ per cent in the effectiveness of angles. The inference is clear; concentrate mainly on the middle until the opening has been made for an angled volley to outspeed the defenders.

There is an additional benefit in that shots down the middle draw the opponents together, so increasing the chances of clashes and misunderstandings. However, the serving pair are also vulnerable in this way so how can this be guarded against?

The answer is relatively simple. Let the man who played the last shot also take the next. Revert to figure 8.3 where the server has run in and volleyed to A. The server should continue moving forward and slightly to the centre, secure in the knowledge that his partner is covering lobs. If the receivers drive for the middle, the server will actually be moving towards the oncoming ball and as he is already in motion, will be better able to deal with the middle ball.

Indeed, it is a good general rule always to move along the same line as your last shot and to take all returns coming between you and your partner unless he specifically shouts 'mine'.

Turning to the server's partner, if he has agreed to cover his own half of the net and all lobs, he should perhaps above all ensure that, so far as is humanly possible, he takes all lobs overhead. Once he begins letting lobs bounce, he is giving the receiver a range. While he takes the ball overhead the receiver cannot gauge the length of his lobs. Even a moderate overhead shot is preferable to letting the ball bounce before replying with, say, a perfect counter-lob.

There is one danger in this system: an inclination to do too little about dealing with returns of service. Even if you have agreed to cover your half of the court and all lobs, always be alert for the chance to nip over and cut off the return of service with a devastating volley. Nothing is more disconcerting to the receiver than an ever-present, nagging fear that his return will be poached and killed.

When you poach there must be no half measures about it. The rally has to end there and then. Obviously there will be a few occasions when it continues: a lucky scrape up, a determined retrieve, perhaps a brilliant counter-volley will keep it going or even cost you the point. Nevertheless, you are the one taking the initiative; you are the pair who will normally–note normally–be out of position, so kill the ball at all costs.

This is psychologically important. Nothing depresses the receiving pair more than a net man who is dealing out destruction right, left and centre. Conversely, they are cheered enormously by a poacher whose volleys are no more decisive than the incoming service. If they are at all experienced, they realise that the risks taken by the server's partner are in no way justified by the gains.

To go back to that word 'normally': loss of position through poaching can be avoided if the server and his partner operate a system of signals telling one another of their intentions. Normally the server's partner should call the play.

Turning his back so the receivers cannot see, he can, for example, point his first finger straight down the handle of his racket to indicate he is going across. Two fingers down the handle might indicate: 'I shall feint as if I'm going across but then go back'.

In the first case the server will veer in his run to cover the

place vacated by his partner. In the second he will carry on un-
checked, relying on his partner to cover the apparent gap he
has left. Each time there is no loss of position by the serving
team.

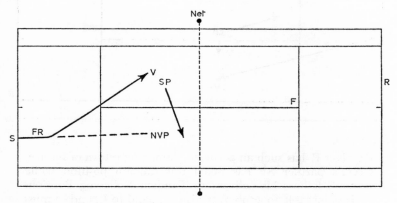

Figure 8.4

How signals affect the server's run in. His partner SP signals
'I'm going across'. S serves the ball to F and sets out along FR.
Just before receiver R hits his return, SP darts diagonally
across while S changes direction and runs in to V. If SP had
signalled: 'I shall feint to go across and then return', S would
have run straight on to NVP.

The partnership can have other signals indicating where to
serve, what spin, speed and, in fact, almost anything. Agree
beforehand if the signal remains operative after a fault and do
first use them in matches against pairs weaker than yourselves.
Until they become second nature, signals are a tax on concentration; it is no use having even the best theoretical plan in creation
if you are so busy thinking about it you fail to put the ball in
play.

There are some men who are so phlegmatic and steady that
nothing breaks the monotonously regular flow of returns which
speed low and fast wide across the court. Against such men it is
sometimes advantageous to use the tandem formation of figure
8.5 in which the server's partner remains on the same side of the

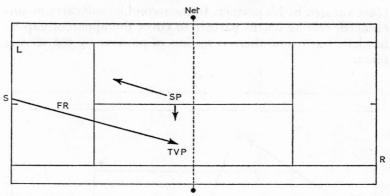

Figure 8.5

Receiver R has such an accurate, damaging return of service, server's partner SP has taken this tandem position while server S follows his delivery to Tandem Volleying Position. SP is vulnerable to a lob over his backhand to L, and so must be ready to dart in either of the directions indicated by the arrow.

court as the server. As most players have a sliced backhand, he is well placed to poach but if the receiver lobs well he will need to be both fast enough to get back and supple enough to smash with the forehand instead of the backhand, normally a shot lacking the finality of a forehand kill. The other asset which should be cultivated by the server's partner is 'the drift'. Based on the outright poach, he continuously eases over towards the middle of the net without finally committing himself, so leaving a gap down the line. This drift normally worries the receiver into placing the ball farther and farther across the court until he begins overshooting the sideline.

All such theoretical knowledge is valuable but there are bound to be days on which you are outgunned by stronger opponents or are below your normal best. On such days one encounters countless difficulties of which none is more frustrating than an inability to stop the receiver returning the ball low and strongly enough to permit his partner to stand close in and poach your first volleys.

In this situation your partner can be of great assistance. You have served, rushed in, scraped over a low volley and are off balance as well as badly positioned and flustered. The receiver's partner has closed in on the net and intercepted your volley. Usually he will aim at the gap and, according to my earlier advice, you should cover the middle. In this situation you won't stand much chance.

However, if your partner is an intelligent 'off the ball' player, he may be able to retrieve the situation by retreating fractionally, keeping his racket up in an alert, ready for action position and by covering the middle.

In such a situation the odds are definitely in favour of the receiver winning the point, but they can be reduced by intelligent anticipation and positioning. The trick is in sensing quickly what is happening, where the ball is likely to go and in covering that place on the court.

By expecting the worst and trying to act accordingly, you do have a slight chance. If you stand by, transfixed and hoping it won't happen, you leave the server unsupported. You lose the point and the server a little more of his confidence.

Once again, the key to success is speed; speed of thought, reaction and counter-action. As in singles, speed is the most important single asset in the game.

9 · More about Doubles Play: Return of Service and Positioning

You and your partner will never lose a doubles match if you never drop your services. Equally, you will never win unless you learn how to break your opponents' service. This puts return of service on a par with service itself so far as importance is concerned.

There is one vital difference between returning service in singles and doubles. In singles length is frequently valuable. In doubles it can never be useful against a class pair, because length is obtained by increasing the clearance of the ball over the net, and that makes volleying easy either for the server running in or for his partner at the net.

Thus the best returns of service are mixtures chopped down from the top of the service's bounce, heavily top spun drives and angled dinks. All of these force the incoming server to volley from below the height of the net. This limits the power of the volley and also gives your partner an opportunity to cut across the net and intercept.

This, however, is running ahead. First consider basic policy. Unless the return of service crosses the net and is going to fall in court, you cannot win the point. Ideally every return of service must be good but life consists of compromises rather than ideals. In returning service, getting the ball back may be at the expense of giving the server and his partner simple returns that they can volley easily for winners.

Against strong opposition, merely putting the ball in play will not suffice. You must accept the risk of missing occasionally in order to protect yourself from having the ball volleyed out of reach. If you actually lose the point, it doesn't matter a great deal if the loss comes on the first (service), third (first volley) or thirty-first shot made by the opposition. The thirty-first is preferable because at least they will have suffered some nerve strain but it is still a lost point.

Jan Kukal and Vladimir Zednik won the King's Cup for

More about Doubles Play

Czechoslovakia in Cologne at the end of 1969 simply by slamming at every service with every ounce of strength. Some 80 per cent never went near the court but their own services were so formidable – both exceed six feet in height by several inches – that they could shelter behind their virtual unbreakability while hoping that every now and then two or three returns might go in, the opponents might double fault and they would get the break and the set. In beating Britain's Peter Curtis and Mark Cox over five sets they served in thirty-four games, losing only two of them. When the mathematics of holding service are, like that example, sixteen to one on, you can afford to 'go for broke' on return of service. But few matches are played on courts as fast as the one in Cologne and not many partnerships aggregate 12 ft. 6 in. of height, so it is preferable, I believe, to seek greater certainty with return of service.

Mobility and speed are other relevant factors. Given the agility and mobility of a Laver or a Chuck McKinley, you can better retrieve difficult situations caused by weak returns than if you are a taller, less mobile man like, say, Clifford Drysdale. However, the sheer speed of Laver and McKinley enables them to make good returns off fast serves that would have put slower men in difficulties.

Against this, the taller man will have an advantage when serving. In fact, of twenty-eight winners of post-war Wimbledon doubles, seventeen men were six feet or more tall and eleven were shorter than six feet. Winners of the French men's doubles championship, which is played on slow hard courts, show a very similar ratio, that is, twenty who were six feet or over to thirteen below six feet.

In singles, the Wimbledon ratio is 11 to 8 and the French is 8 to 8.

Thus it seems there is a slight advantage in being tall in doubles on all surfaces and in singles on fast courts, but in singles on slow courts the mobility of a smaller man neutralises the power of the six footer.

Viewed mathematically, there is a 50 per cent advantage in being six feet tall or over, but the number of winners in both singles and doubles who are below six feet proves that this is by no means an insuperable barrier.

The tall man's advantage lies in power, so that it is necessary for the smaller man to exploit to the limit his superior mobility in doubles, whether on grass or hard courts.

In returning service in doubles, dinks, top spins and lobs should be your main attacking weapons. 'Never' springs to mind when considering the ordinary flat drive. Yet it must be used fairly frequently, if only by way of contrast.

The dink is a softish shot taken while the service ball is still rising and angled away to the singles sideline as near to the net as possible. Its object is to force the server to volley or half volley upwards off his toes. Because he will be close to the net, his shot cannot be powerful. If the ball evades your partner posted near the net, you will be able to volley it for you will have had sufficient time to run forward to a volleying position yourself. The only danger in dinking is that if the shot is too soft, the ball will bounce so high that the server will be able to pause on his run in and make a murderous drive from half-way up the service court off a ball above net height. Hit at, say, 60 m.p.h., such a drive will reach the receiver's partner in about one-tenth of a second, which does not allow him much time to react and move.

The top spin drive fulfils a similar purpose, but it will pitch slightly deeper in court and, because the ball travels faster, allow the receiver less time to follow his return into the net.

A normal flat drive will pitch even deeper in court and allow even less time for the receiver to follow in. Nevertheless, it has to be used extensively to prevent the dink and the top spin becoming expected routine.

Occasionally the receiver should lob over the man at the net, especially if he shows any tendency to drift or poach.

All these returns imply that the server will consistently put over a fastish ball that pitches near the junction of the centre and service lines. In fact he will not, so there is another return which should be used occasionally and that is a flat drive down the server's partner's sideline. At worst such returns will help to keep him in his place when you are receiving and at best will win the point outright because he has moved over too quickly and too far in his effort to poach.

When returning service try to outsmart the server and his partner. . . . But with your brain, not just with your eye. Watch the service preparation very carefully because you will find nine servers out of ten possess 'give away' habits that can tell you in advance where they are going to place the ball.

From the moment the ball leaves the server's hand, glue your eye to it. You know, perhaps, that because it is a little to the server's right he is going to slice the ball wide to your forehand (you are in the right-hand court) and you recall that the last twice he did this his partner darted across the net to intercept your return with a volley winner. So as the ball reaches you, you aim your return down his sideline AND you act on the assumption that the man at the net will not cut across. Providing your return is low and fast his chances of making a volley winner will not be too great.

Your pay-off can come the next time your opponent serves to the forehand. His partner, having poached successfully twice and then not gone across when you aimed for his sideline, will be 80 per cent certain to try to poach the next time and the point will be yours outright.

Understand that this is a simple example. It is given as an indication of the way to think when receiving service, while at the same time never taking your eyes off the ball.

The lines and the net don't move. The opponents do move. Memorise, till it is second nature, exactly where the net band and sidelines are in relation to every height of ball in all positions on your court, and watch the ball like a hawk while using the net band and sidelines as mental sighters. When this becomes completely automatic your brain will be free to outthink both men across the net.

Because time is so important in doubles, you should stand closer in to receive service than in singles. Apart from saving time, this will result in your taking the ball at a greater height off the ground. This greater height plus a more advanced receiving position will increase the angles open to you and so enable you to harass the serving team more effectively.

Whenever the server faults, move in a couple of paces for the second service. Learn to crowd the ball. Roll with the server's throw up to indicate you are seeking to run round the ball and crush the service with your forehand. Stand right in occasionally to receive first service. Do anything feasible within the laws of the game to menace the server, but realise it all involves risk. Usually of losing the point, occasionally of looking foolish as well. But risk is an occupational hazard of all sports. Learn to calculate the risks. Think, think, think all the time.

Diagram 9.1 illustrates all the points made in the text.

All these theories hold good for the left court but there are slight practical differences. First, most services will be angled to the backhand rather than down the centre line. Second, any interceptions by server's partner will entail use of his backhand volley. This reduces his reach a little, though this may be partly cancelled out because most backhand volleys are struck a little more in advance of the body than forehand volleys. This makes the angle of cover similar for forehand and backhand whether intercepting in right or left court, but in the left court his slight increase in reach gives the server's partner added protection on the right, so making a down-the-line return of service slightly more hazardous.

Third, because the cross-court return of service must be widely angled in order to evade the server's partner at the net, the ball has farther to travel and this gives the server's partner a fraction longer to think and act.

All these factors make bigger differences in theory than in reality, but it is true that in men's doubles there is slightly more poaching in the left court than in the right.

Diagram 9.2 shows the possibilities. Of these, G and H, the lobs, need more explanation. Because the server's partner is already on the net, the obvious lob is over his head to area G, but this is over his forehand kill. So the lob must be long and should be a surprise.

The lob to H, over the server's head, is one of the most devastating in tennis, and also one of the most difficult shots of all to execute.

There is a general point to be made about lobbing, whether in singles or doubles, whether returning service or in rally play.

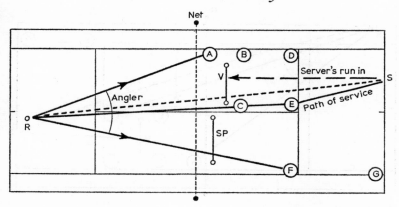

Figure 9.1

Return of service possibilities. S serves along the dotted line and runs in to where the line V shows his position and reach. The line SP shows his partner's position and reach.

The dotted line shows the path of the service to R. Angle r covers the choice of returns.

A is the area for a dink, B and C the areas for a top-spin drive, D and E the areas for a flat drive. All these are beyond the reach of SP unless he drifts to the right or goes for a full interception. Unless he does, a return towards area F will present him with a volley, but if he tries to intercept, this return will win the point outright.

A lob to G will cause great difficulty if it is a surprise, and it may sometimes do so even when it is not a surprise, if it is perfectly flighted for length and height.

The farther forward R can make his return, the more angle r increases and the less time there is for the serving team to establish position.

Conversely, the more R retreats, the more time he gives the serving team and the less angle r becomes.

So it is, on balance, advantageous to sacrifice some power when returning service in order to take the ball nearer the net.

This is that 90 per cent of tennis players, even those in the championship class, generally lob too late and when it is obvious they are going to do so. They regard the lob as a defensive stroke, and, of course, it often is just that.

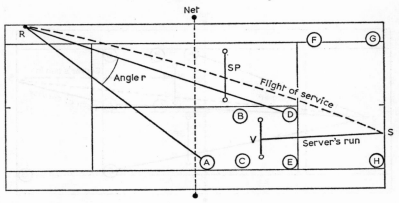

Figure 9.2

S = server; SP = reach of server's partner; V = reach of server after running in; R = receiver.

Possible returns of service:

A = dink area

B and C = areas of top spin drives

D and E = areas for flat drives. Note SP covers D without moving

F = area for down-the-line return

G and H = areas for lobs

But it can and should be an offensive weapon, used especially when an opponent has been manoeuvred out of a position he is hurrying to regain. In doubles this might be brought about by a top spin return down the middle, which forces a moderately defensive half volley, also down the middle. Maybe a volley or drive into the gap will win the point. A low, fastish lob over the spot he has just vacated will do so almost, if not quite, as often; and it will also build up the points won by aiming at the gap, for he will never be sure whether to cover the gap and risk the lob, or to anticipate the lob and not close the gap completely.

The essence of good tactics is surprise, and the attacking lob is an ace of surprise. It is, of course, a difficult shot to acquire for it demands sound judgment, good technique and a refined touch. Yet at the start of the 1970s top stars like Laver, Rosewall, Newcombe and Roche are reaping rich rewards for the hours they have spent developing this shot.

More about Doubles Play

As with the serving team, off the ball positioning is tremendously important, so where should the receiver's partner stand during the serve–return of serve opening of each point?

Much will depend on the relative strengths of the server and the receiver. You may be the quickest racket mover in the world but if the server is thundering over deliveries which are forcing short lobs that the server and his partner are killing with 100 m.p.h. ferocity, you are wasting time and endangering your personal safety by taking up a position close to the net.

On the other hand, if your partner is tormenting the server unendurably with his dinks and top spin returns, you are not only letting the server off the hook, but destroying your partner's morale at the same time, by failing to take up a net position from which you menace the server even if you don't actually intercept.

So the receiver's partner's position depends on three variables:
(1) The strength of the service and first volley.
(2) The effectiveness of the returner of service.
(3) The reflexes and volleying skill of the receiver's partner.

While it is stupid to stand close in and have the ball drilled through you by the incoming volleyer, it must never be forgotten that ninety-nine out of every hundred men's doubles are won by the attacking pair.

Consequently, when it is a close call between adventure and safety first, elect to be adventurous. Apart from the tactical rightness of this attitude, it is also psychologically correct. Adventure is stimulating and it breeds optimism. Safety first is, in the end, self-diminishing; it may win a close first set but is unlikely to prevail in a critical final set.

The optimum court position of the receiver's partner, then, is somewhere between the service line and about one-third of the way up the service court–even closer in if the server is weak, the returner of service very strong, or there is a combination of both.

It should never be so far forward that you have to move diagonally backwards when drifting towards the middle of the court or positively darting across to intercept the first or subsequent volley.

If you intercept and the server or server's partner scrapes the ball back, you are better able to make yet another telling volley

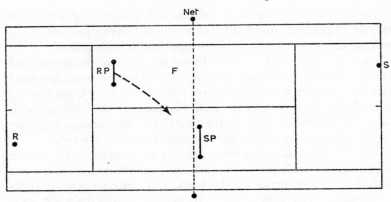

Figure 9.3

S = server; SP = net cover of server's partner; R = receiver;
RP = coverage of receiver's partner.

From the position shown, RP has a fraction longer to see
what is happening and in intercepting can move diagonally
forward, so moving on to the ball while giving himself room to
swerve or otherwise adjust position.

At F, unless he is ultra-quick, he will have to move at best
in a straight line across court and at worst diagonally backwards, so losing power and increasing the chances of erring.

if you are in forward motion than if you are retreating slightly.
The mental attitude of successful volleying and intercepting is
one of aggression, of going forward, not of backing away from
the action.

Earlier I advocated volleying deep down the middle until you
have created the opening for a winning angled volley. In poaching that opening may be immediately available because the
opponent 'off the ball' should, if he is alert, move quickly to
cover the gap. Therefore a volley hit behind him may well beat
him by yards. And, remember, when you intercept you must do
so with complete determination to end the rally immediately.

Once the rally has passed one of the conventional three or
four shot openings, the possibilities become infinite. Speed on the
ball is decisive, but this must be learned on the practice court.

Skilled positioning and covering are worth many points a
match. This knowledge comes mainly from match play. You

can develop understanding with a partner while practising, but it needs match play to get the pair of you thinking as one. When you think as one, you will automatically move in unison to bisect all angles open to the opponent playing the ball.

There should be no 'Sorries' between two good partners. Each man should know that the other is trying to the limits of his capabilities, so that if he makes a silly mistake he will be angrier about it than you.

Therefore it is up to each partner always to encourage the other. Not profusely nor too obviously but quietly and sincerely. Forget how brilliant *you* are; it won't mean a thing if your partner is off form and you lose. In doubles, cease thinking individually; instead, sublimate your individuality for the good of the pair.

Never fall into that all too common, unmannerly habit of going around the court wearing a look of 'how can he (my partner) do this to me?' No one is fooled by it. Your personal ego is unimportant; you win or lose as a pair.

Learn to think for the pair, not as an individual. Bring out the best in your partners, and soon you will be the most sought doubles player in your club, county or even country.

More importantly, you will derive so much more pleasure from your tennis even in 'Open' tournaments when considerable money is at stake.

Maybe it is an old-fashioned idea, but I believe pleasure to be as vital as cash, and further, that it can itself be the means of gathering greater financial rewards from tennis.

That is why training and tactics have value in themselves, irrespective of external rewards. Happiness is an elusive quality. Seek it deliberately and it will often elude you. Immerse yourself completely in some activity–for instance, in improving your tennis by training assiduously–and after some months or years you will realise you have been too much involved for such abstract ideas as happiness to enter your head yet you have been supremely happy all the same. As I have written before, to travel hopefully is better than to arrive. If this book leads to a few hopeful tennis journeys, I shall be well satisfied.

10 · Personality Factors

A long-term study of middle-distance runners shows that they tend, over the years, to change personality. Like most athletes, they begin as marked extroverts but slowly move along the continuum towards introversion as they become better performers.[1]

Of all running events, middle-distance races make the severest demands on tactics. So they bear some resemblance to tennis, certainly sufficient to postulate that personality changes do take place over a period of years in men and women who really strive to advance.

Whether or not it is possible to know oneself too thoroughly is debatable. So far as tennis players are concerned, the subject has been covered in one book[2] and one magazine article.[3] Here it is sufficient to say that extroversion v. introversion, casualness v. conscientiousness, toughness v. sensitivity and anxiety v. serenity are key factors.

Strangely, there is absolutely no correlation between I.Q. and tennis know-how. The *Lawn Tennis* magazine research of 1965 produced a perfect 'scatter' and other researches have duplicated the findings.

Nervousness is one of the fruits of anxiety. You should, of course, be nervous when you walk on court. If you are not you are not really keyed up sufficiently to bring out your best form.

On the other hand, that nervousness should disappear within moments of the match starting. If it does not there is something wrong with your philosophy of tennis and, to some extent, of life itself.

There is, surely, only one reasonable thing to hope for when playing a match and that is to maintain the best form of which

[1] John Kane, C.C.P.R. 'Fitness for Sport' Conference, January 1965.

[2] *Tennis: How to Become a Champion* by C. M. Jones (Faber and Faber).

[3] Article by John Kane and John Callaghan, *British Lawn Tennis*, July 1965.

you are capable. The chances of exceeding that form are very remote.

To attain that form your mind must be completely freed of doubts. It is useless regretting the late night party of last night or the night before when you are tiring at four games all in the final set. Better to have exercised some discipline and passed up the party for a quiet evening followed by adequate rest. In truth, the party may have had little or no physical effect but that is not the thing that counts. It is the psychological effect which is decisive. From four-all onwards there is simply no room in the mind for doubts or distractions. Your opponent will be putting forth his greatest efforts and you will need every scrap of mental and physical endurance you possess in order to stay with him and eventually win.

Inhibition lessens effort, as anyone who has seen the phenomenal strength of madmen must know. There is no room for needless inhibitions set up by poor preparation, either in training or in on-court practice.

However, despite perfect preparation and an ideal attitude during your match you may still lose.

On the positive side, you cannot have any possible reason for self-reproach. You have done everything possible, played the best tennis of which you are capable, and still lost.

Disappointment is understandable and determination essential. The hard fact is that the other man is currently a better player. The determination is needed to redouble your efforts in practice, especially the quality of your practice. For quality of effort rather than quantity is what achieves improvement.

This is where conscientiousness and toughness come in. Toughness is needed to maintain the detailed practice which brings advancement. Conscientiousness discovers the points that are weak and devises means of correction.

In all this, an ability to face and come to terms with defeat must be achieved. Note 'to come to terms'. This does not mean to accept defeat as a permanent state, a habit. Because losing can become a habit, just as winning can.

The first step is to face the worst, namely that you may lose to your deadly rival. Ask yourself squarely 'what would be all the worst aspects of defeat?' Write them down and study them.

Then decide what action you will take to counter those effects.

Having faced the worst and decided what you will do, relegate it all to the back of your mind and concentrate instead on all the things which can help you beat him.

Imagine yourself playing and winning. Build up a clear picture of victory. Mentally rehearse your methods because mental rehearsal is a proven path to improvement.[1]

This exercise demands great powers of concentration and self-discipline. Day dreaming will not suffice. It must be ordered, intense application to the task as it will be. If successful, you will probably start nervously. This should not but nevertheless may persist.

There are several practical ways of combating nervousness. The first is to control your breathing. Draw in long and slowly, hold the air for a second or so and then exhale quickly. Repeat at least six times. Take your time between points while carrying out this exercise.

Another practical method is to concentrate your mind on finding some new facet of your opponent's game. Look to see how the direction of his backhand returns varies according to the height he takes the ball or how the direction of his forehand drive can be judged from the position of his feet or . . . but there are so many things to look for.

Appear calm at all times no matter what turmoil is going on within. People will tell you you are calm and in a while, two years maybe, you will believe yourself to be calm. We all become more like the image we show to others.

Consider that if you are nervous your opponent is probably suffering just as badly. The *Lawn Tennis* research revealed that all players are nervous. Where champions differ from non-champions is in their ability to control those nerves.

Maybe it will affect your wind. Breathe deeply. Perhaps your arms and legs will stiffen—you will get the 'steel elbow'. If so, consciously set yourself to relaxing. Take your time between the points and 'think' relaxation, beginning at the toes and working upwards.

Routine well established is a great antidote, for it gives you

[1] C. M. Jones, *op. cit.*

subconsciously something to cling to when the mind starts freezing. This is one of the reasons why the Guards are drilled and drilled and drilled. When the going is terrifying and the mind freezes, the nerves and body will, if necessary, work almost independently of all else if the drill has been sufficiently intensive and long.

Back in the 1956 Wimbledon singles semi-finals Angela Buxton reached match point against Patricia Ward. She was almost paralysed with nerves but she had practised ten thousand times a 'serve to the backhand, backhand to the forehand corner and up to the net for a winning volley' routine. She used it . . . and Miss Ward was also so nervous she did not get anywhere near the backhand down-the-line bit of the sequence. Practice for Miss Buxton had brought a machine-like efficiency that went beyond the control of nervousness.

Another factor which should encourage you is the thought that your opponent may be as nervous as you. If he is not, he is not fully attuned to make a major effort.

According to your basic personality, the manner of your nervousness will vary. Without in any way yielding to it, accept that you will be or are nervous, and then think positively about conquering your opponent.

Be a perfectionist who will not be satisfied with poor performance. This acceptance of poor performance, this lack of pride, has been an unwelcome feature of British tennis for almost two decades. Obviously, there have been notable exceptions, but, possibly because of the relative ease with which a living can be made and a gay social life enjoyed, too many outstanding prospects have never approached anything like their full potential.

David McClelland, a Harvard psychologist, has isolated an important factor of personality which he has named 'The self-motivated urge to achieve'. He has given it the symbol 'N.ach'. This appears strongly only in a very small proportion of people, who are driven by this inner force to do any task to the limits of their possibilities, whether it be playing a complicated game like tennis or sweeping a floor.

It is not a trait which makes for great happiness. Yet it shows up in very young children with some clarity. Lack of it can be gathered from various clues. For example, men and women with a high N.ach measure seldom have more than a passing interest in gambling.

All this would be only of academic interest had Professor McClelland not said that this urge to achieve, to attain perfection, can be acquired, at least partially, by those who lack it naturally. As consultant to I.B.M. in America, he has devised techniques for measuring achievement potential. More importantly, he has produced courses which improve or develop this factor, and I.B.M. are using them effectively, especially at middle management levels.

Such courses are still relatively in their infancy, and it is difficult to see how a normal tennis player can gain entry to them. Nevertheless, mere realisation of the N.ach factor, and an understanding that it can be improved, are important.

Nature has equipped us with a N.ach quota and the ability to reach a certain position but we are also creatures of free will. Therefore, our position and quota of N.ach are not fixed for all time. We can, if we have sufficient determination and persistence, improve both these abstract factors just as much as we improve the more obvious things like an unreliable forehand or defensive backhand.

The road to success is on the practice court and the training gymnasium. Mental fitness is, perhaps, more nebulous than physical fitness, and so harder to measure. Too much tournament play undoubtedly weakens it, just as too little develops it insufficiently.

Nothing that I can think of can be more competitive and nerve-testing than flying a bomber in war. The Royal Air Force made and maintained continuous and detailed studies of such air-crew during World War II. They discovered many vital trends and tendencies including:

(a) Performance rose during the first few operational missions and then tailed away markedly towards the end of the normal thirty operations.
(b) Body weight followed a similar curve and was reflected by—
(c) A marked rise in psychiatric disorders which only rest cured.

Personality Factors

(d) The performance and morale of each member of a crew had an immense effect on all others in it.

These were, of course, statistical generalities that varied from man to man. Yet translated into tennis terms, it suggests that improvement of mind, body and technique demands great skill and considerable self-discipline. In particular, a well adjusted balance between tournaments, practice and rest must be found and morale must be kept high. Enthusiastic, hard working, cheerful companions help here and action is the great antidote to depression, lack of confidence and so on.

If you run into a period of self doubt, remember how Jonah Barrington began press-ups in the shower minutes after his agonisingly disappointing defeat by Cam Nancarrow in the 1968 inaugural World Championships of Squash Rackets. There was no guarantee he would fare any better in the future but there was only one way to try and that was by making an even bigger effort, so why delay?

Incidentally, he felt himself lower in the 'pecking order' than both Cam Nancarrow and Geoff Hunt. Realising it, he accepted the fact that these men had superior technical ability and could, at times, make him look foolish. Intense self-discipline enabled him to ride out the latter factor in subsequent meetings and he set about neutralising their superior technical skills by developing his tactical ingenuity and physical fitness.

His revenge over Nancarrow in the 1969 World Championships and his win over Hunt in the final of the 1969 English Open Championship prove that will power and self-discipline can move a person up from the position he feels has been assigned to him by nature, perhaps permanently, for Barrington no longer feels any personal inferiority to either man, even though he accepts their superior abilities as actual timers and hitters of the ball.

His advance indicates great toughness of mind and it is a fact established beyond question by the *Lawn Tennis* personality research that the Australian players are, as a group, one standard deviation tougher than any other ethnic group.

As an extremely rough and ready test, take the simple test

121

which ends this chapter. It is little more than a party game, but it will indicate tendencies.

Confidence is a vital factor in tennis; but supreme physical fitness is also an enormous help. The knowledge that one can stay on court all day without tiring, can react and move swiftly, and can twist and turn in all directions – that one possesses all-round flexibility – completely removes doubt about one aspect of one's game. And doubt is a major enemy of confidence.

Winning is largely a state of mind. Maureen Connolly, probably the greatest woman player in history, had the right approach. 'I aim to perfect my game,' she told me once. 'If my game becomes perfect I will beat everybody.'

Putting winning first is sometimes taken to indicate a good supply of 'killer instinct'. This is a popular belief, but how much truth is there in it?

Professor H. J. Eysenck, the world famous psychologist, dealt with this subject in a definitive article which he wrote specially for *Lawn Tennis* magazine. Entitled 'Fact and Fiction of Killer Instinct', it read:

'It is often said of tennis players who do not quite come up to the highest expectations that they lack the "killer instinct". Christine Truman is sometimes given as an example, or in earlier days Bunny Austin. Is there really such a thing as a "killer instinct"; is it a desirable quality; and if so, can it be cultivated? Questions of this kind are often put to a professional psychologist like myself who is interested in tennis and has played and watched it all his life. I am not sure that any very certain answers can be given, but there are a number of facts available which may help one look at the whole problem with some greater insight than before.

'The main characteristic of the person who has the killer instinct is presumably his unusually strong drive and motivation to succeed. Let us assume that this is so and ask just what is known about the relationship between drive and success at any task requiring skill. The general formula which psychologists have found to hold true over a wide range of skill is: $P = D \times H$, meaning that performance is a function of habit multiplied by drive or motivation. Habit, in this context, means the sum of those skills which the person has acquired in the past through assiduous practice; in the case of tennis they include such things as the ability to hit a service with any desired degree of speed or slice to any desired part of the opponent's court; to hit forehand or precision backhand with a given speed, angle, and precision; to anticipate your opponent's reaction; to pace your game throughout the match and raise it when necessary, and so forth. These habits may be taken as given once you are in a match; you are not likely to improve them during the short period of time the match lasts. Consequently, it would seem that the most important variable, given a particular set of habits acquired through prior practice, is the amount of drive which is present, and if the man with the killer instinct is indeed characterised by the exceptionally high drive, then it would appear that he must come out as favourite, given equal skill in habits.

'Unfortunately (or fortunately) the simple picture is vastly oversimplified and does not take into account one of the oldest and most firmly established laws in psychology, the so called Yerkes-Dodson law. This law, which was discovered eight years before I was born and is therefore of considerable antiquity, has two parts. The first part states that performance improves with increase in drive, but only up to a certain point; beyond this optimum an increase in drive is accompanied by a decrement in performance. The second part of the law states that the more difficult the task is, the lower is the optimum drive level. Considering that tennis is a highly skilled game in which many very difficult shots have to be attempted in order to overcome an opponent of roughly equal skill, this would suggest that the optimum drive level in tennis is relatively low, so that the killer instinct would be a handicap rather than a help. Is this in fact so?

'In order to answer this question, let us first enquire why the relationship between drive and performance is curvilinear rather than straight forward. There are several reasons, but I shall only mention two. In the first place any particular situation in life tends to call forth not just one habit but a whole series of competing habits. My opponent has hit a half volley to my forehand and has come up to the net: I could try to pass him down the forehand line; I could lob him on the same side, or to his forehand; or I could try a cross-court pass shot, hoping that this will surprise him into making a mistake. A strong drive will power all these habits, but most of all the one which is most firmly established, which quite likely will be the cross-court shot. Under the particular circumstances, however, this may be the wrong choice and it might be better to bring into action a habit much lower in the hierarchy, such as a lob. If drive is not very strong then the performance potential of these various habits will not differ too widely and the player can make a reasonable choice. If the drive is very strong however, then multiplying it by a strong habit makes the combination predominate so much over all other alternatives that a proper, rational choice becomes difficult or impossible, and the wrong shot will be played.

'Another reason for the decrement in performance with very high drives is the presence of what are called "drive stimuli". If you are very hungry, then you are working under a strong drive. You are also conscious, however, of certain stimuli such as hunger pangs in your stomach which are associated with this drive and which have in the past been associated with certain courses of action, such as the seeking for food. If you are playing tennis at the time you might think that a strong hunger drive would be helpful because it increases the total amount of drive present, but of course, the drive stimuli (hunger pangs) act as a distraction and invigorate irrelevant habits which interfere with your proper game.

'This may seem farfetched, but let us suppose that you are playing under a strong emotional drive to win at all costs. This is accompanied by certain drive stimuli such as an increase in heart rate, an outpouring of adrenalin into the bloodstream, an increase in breathing rate, a drying up of the digestive juices, and many more. These drive stimuli have in the past been associated with aggression, hatred, and other similar emotions, and consequently they will tend to encourage habits appropriate to these emotions. For instance they might lead you to hit the ball furiously hard at your opponent when a delicate drop shot might have been much more effective. Indeed, the term "killer instinct" implies a perfect recognition of these facts; the drive stimuli you are experiencing are precisely those which you would experience if you hated your opponent and wanted to kill him! But killing your opponent is one thing; beating him at tennis is another; and the habits appropriate to the former task are inappropriate for the latter and interfere with it, so that performance suffers.

'Is the killer instinct then entirely a bad thing? That would be going too far. In addition to skill, other things are involved in tennis such as persistence, endurance, and simple physical exertion. These are all in part dependent on certain special physical reactions of the organism sometimes called the "fight or flight" syndrome, which is described elsewhere. Your heart beats faster, so that more oxygen can course through the body; your breathing rate goes up for the same reason. Your digestion stops in order to make blood available for the brain and the rest of the body. Thus the killer instinct would make you into a more efficient fighting machine from the simple point of view of physical strength and endurance, and this may be an important consideration in a long drawn-out five-set match. Ideally, one might say that both extremes are probably to be avoided. The player with too much killer instinct will deprive himself of his more skilful and complex shots and will be distracted by irrelevant habits; the "desiccated calculating machine" will be better able to make use of his appropriate habits, and play more skilfully, but may wither in the heat of a long protracted battle. The optimum point is probably a strong desire to win, sufficiently to produce some of the "fight or flight" reactions but not to an extent that would interfere with the deployment of higher-order skills. The optimum point of compromise will probably differ from person to person, but personally I would doubt very much if either Bunny Austin or Christine Truman would benefit from the possession of the killer instinct; it would more likely have destroyed the whole basis of their game and made them less efficient players – as well as less nice people!'

Before moving on, take this rough test to gain some idea of whether or not you possess sufficient toughness for top tennis. Though not especially proven, it will give an approximation to fact. Remember, it is not essential to be mentally tough but it does make the demanding nature of practice and training that much easier.

THE TEST

1. My friends believe my heart rules my head.
   a) True   b) perhaps   c) false

2. I am more interested in religious matters than in politics.
   a) true   b) not sure   c) false

3. I would enjoy running a medium-sized business more than being a member of a group.
   a) true   b) uncertain   c) false

4. Do you complain to the head waiter if you are served with poor food in a restaurant?
   a) yes   b) sometimes   c) never

5. I admire Plato more than I do Henry Ford.
   a) true   b) uncertain   c) false

6. I am more interested in improved productivity than in a unified religious creed.
   a) true   b) uncertain   c) false

7. I greatly enjoy a TV show of the 'I love Lucy' or 'Sunday Night at the Palladium' type.
   a) true   b) in between   c) false

8. Pride rides before a fall so you enjoy seeing dignitaries and intellectuals having their dignity upset.
   a) true   b) uncertain   c) false

9. I feel that many of my friends are less sensitive than I to the artistic side of life.
   a) true   b) uncertain   c) false

10. I enjoy daydreaming.
    a) yes   b) uncertain   c) no

So much for temperament and mental training. Now let us turn to what many will consider a less complicated and more practical field–physical training.

COULD YOU BE A CHAMPION?
Key to the test on page 126

1. a, 0; b, 1; c, 2.	6. a, 0; b, 1; c, 2.
2. a, 2; b, 1; c, 0.	7. a, 0; b, 1; c, 2.
3. a, 0; b, 1; c, 2.	8. a, 0; b, 1; c, 2.
4. a, 0; b, 1; c, 2.	9. a, 2; b, 1; c, 0.
5. a, 2; b, 1; c, 0.	10. a, 2; b, 1; c, 0.

On no account read this until you have completed the questionnaire on page 126 and discovered your score.

Your score does not prove that you are right or wrong but it does indicate your position on a continuum stretching from extreme tough-mindedness, self-reliance and realism to tender-minded, sensitive dependence.

A score from 0–4 suggests exceptional tough-mindedness, from 5–8 above average tough-mindedness, from 9–13 a normal balance between tough and tender-mindedness, from 14–17 above average tenderness and 18–20 extreme tenderness. The composite champion averages 8 but one all-time 'great' was right down at 5.

11 · Physical Fitness

The preceding chapters should have convinced you that good tactical methods demand great strength of will backed by outstanding fitness. To a great extent the two go together, for nothing saps will-power more than uncertainty and tiredness. If you are fit you know that you cannot be broken physically, whatever else may happen. Determination is aided, as Tony Trabert unconsciously revealed after winning the Wimbledon singles in 1955. Supremely fit, he said: 'I did not care if I had to stay on the court until dark, I was determined to come off it the winner.'

So before delving into the practicalities of training, try to understand fully the theory, or at least some of it.

First, what are the objects of training? It has two main goals.

The first is an increase in efficiency. As in stroke practice, you should strive to achieve smoother, more economical movements. Head rolling, arm wobbling, leg jerking and so on detract from speed and balance so they should be eliminated. Muscular propulsion during acceleration must be smoothed, rather as perfect carburation improves combustion in a petrol engine. Strength with minimum strain has to be maximised. The faults which hinder this can be helped through improved techniques.

The second is physical development. The heart beat should be strengthened and slowed, the oxygen uptake increased, the joints made more flexible—a stiff ankle joint can reduce reach at the net by six inches or even more. The muscles should be made supple and, if possible, strengthened and improved in the rate of extension and contraction; power, which represents speed on the tennis court, is dependent on muscular 'explosive power'.

As a help in understanding the physiology of training, the following treatise, *The Physiology of Exercise and of Fitness*, by Dr. N. C. C. Sharp of the Department of Experimental Medicine at the University of Glasgow, which was published in the July,

August and September 1968 issues of *Lawn Tennis*, is worth
close perusal.

The series of articles was introduced by M. H. A. Eggleton,
the 1960 R.A.F. squash champion, and was orientated towards
that game, which, in effect, is a speeded up variety of tennis as
far as its physical demands are concerned. The articles are
quoted in their entirety omitting the introduction.

'Physical fitness for squash comprises primarily three factors.
These are stamina, strength and speed. In addition, some other
attributes are essential, particularly agility, balance, muscular
co-ordination and fast reflexes. The gain and development of all
these facets are principally decided by the practice and training
methods tailored to the individual.

'The physiological aspects of, particularly, stamina and
strength, that is, the events and changes within the body, are
discussed in the following paragraphs.

'As can be seen from the table below, squash is a sport with a
particularly high rate of energy expenditure, hence physical
considerations weigh comparatively heavily.

SPORT OR ACTIVITY	ENERGY EXPENDITURE IN KILOCALORIES PER MINUTE
Darts	2·8
Archery	3·5
Cricket	4·8
Golf	5·1
Table-tennis	5·2
Swimming	5·8
Dancing	5·9
Hill-walking	6·2
Sailing	8·7
Hill-climbing	9·4
Football	10·6
Running	13·2
Squash	15·3

'As a general comparison, the F.A.O. recommendation for a
65 kg. man aged 25, living in a temperate climate, is 3,200 kcal.
per day, based on an estimated requirement of:

      Sleep   500 kcal. (1·0/min.)
      Work   1,200 kcal. (2·5/min.)
      Remainder 1,500 kcal. (3·1/min.)

(The results are from the physiology department of the University of Edinburgh. Obviously, for critical analysis, one would wish to know a lot more about the conditions under which they were obtained, but they are included simply as a rough comparison. In particular, values for squash considerably higher than 15·3 kcals./minutes have been obtained.)

'Physical exercise involves mainly the following organs and tissues: the lungs; the haemoglobin in red blood cells; the blood vessels – particularly small arteries, and capillaries; and the muscle cells. In addition, the large amount of heat generated during exercise must be removed, or heat stroke would quickly result, and, over a period of months, body weight may change.

'*The lungs* In the alveoli or air-sacs of these, the gas exchange occurs; oxygen is absorbed from the inspired air, and carbon dioxide is released. At rest, a man breathes six to eight litres of air per minute, from which he extracts about one-third of a litre of oxygen. During maximum exertion the oxygen requirement may rise 20 times, when over 100 litres of air may be breathed per minute, with the extraction of over five litres of oxygen (up to six has been recorded). The maximum amount of oxygen absorbed is controlled by the rate at which the heart can pump the blood through the lungs, rather than by the capacity of the lungs, although this does play some part.

'Since, unlike the situation with regard to food, the body has no appreciable oxygen store (only enough for approximately 20 seconds of moderate activity), it must in exertion very greatly increase the intake and distribution of oxygen in a very short space of time – literally within seconds. The all-importance of oxygen is that it is essential for almost all of the release of energy from food chemicals within the cell (one litre of oxygen liberates about five kilocalories of energy).

'The stimulus to increase the rate and depth of breathing is mainly associated with the great increase in the amount of carbon dioxide diffusing into the blood from the active muscles, and stimulating the brain's respiratory centre, which controls breathing.

'A major physical effort *can* be performed without taking in any more oxygen, as in the case of a short sprint. However, one breathes heavily afterwards! Such an effort is possible due to the body's ability to incur an "oxygen debt".

'The oxygen debt is made possible by the ability of the skeletal muscles to store oxygen (in myoglobin, discussed below) against a short term physical emergency. Myoglobin is the muscles' equivalent of a submarine's batteries; both have to be recharged—the "debt" has to be paid. The table below, Columns 2 and 3, indicates the sites and magnitude of oxygen storage within the body.

Table showing the oxygen stores of an 'untrained' 70 kilogram young man

HOW STORED	WHERE STORED	QUANTITY (militres of oxygen)	PERCENTAGE (of total store)
Haemoglobin	Venous blood	600	38
	Arterial blood	280	18
Myoglobin	Muscle	240	16
Physical solution	Tissue fluid	56	4
Gas	Lungs	370	24

'From the table one can see that the total quantity of oxygen in the body at any given time amounts to little more than a few breaths. One acquires an oxygen debt during the first few rallies of a squash match. When the debt has stopped increasing, the term "second-wind" applies, in which one is in a physiological steady-state and feels subjectively better.

'*The heart* In the resting adult, the heart pumps about five litres of blood per minute. This can be increased to twenty-five litres during exercise. The increase is produced in two ways:

1. the heart rate can be increased up to three times the resting value, up to a useful maximum of about 150 per minute (the rate *can* rise to over 200)
2. the "stroke-volume"—the amount pumped by each beat— can be doubled, from a normal of 60 to 80 ml. up to 120 ml.

'There is some evidence that athletes can increase their stroke volume more readily than untrained people.

'The chief limitation to the rate of exercise is the output of the heart. The heart itself is simply a large hollow muscle, divided by valves into two pairs of smoothly lined compartments. With exercise, the heart increases its mass in the same way that skeletal muscles enlarge, and it can then pump a greater output for a longer time. In general, the well-exercised heart beats more slowly at rest than the "normal", for example Ron Clarke's resting pulse rate at sea level is 28 per minute, compared to a mode of between 70 and 80.

'It is interesting that, in comparison to skeletal muscle, heart muscle seems to be incapable of working without oxygen, that is, it cannot acquire an oxygen debt. This lends support to the belief that one cannot "strain" an initially healthy heart, no matter how intense the exercise—as just mentioned it is the heart which controls the rate of activity, not vice-versa.

'*Haemoglobin* is a compound containing iron, and it is found in the red blood cells. Its purpose is to carry oxygen, in a loose combination, from the lungs to the tissues. By means of haemoglobin the blood can transport 100 times as much oxygen as it could if the oxygen were simply dissolved in the fluid plasma of the blood (the heart would then need to pump 60 litres of blood per minute, instead of 5, even at rest).

'Under normal circumstances, arterial blood contains about 18 per cent of oxygen by volume, combined with haemoglobin. Venous blood similarly contains about 12 per cent.

'During hard exercise, haemoglobin gives up more oxygen than normal, and the venous blood level can drop to as low as 3 per cent.

'In exercise, the circulatory system helps by changing the pattern of the blood flow, that is, by diverting blood away from organs which are not connected with the exercise to the muscles which are involved. When the body is at rest, muscle tissue accounts for about 20 per cent of the absorbed oxygen (about 60 ml.–300 ml. being the resting total body oxygen intake per minute). However, during hard exercise, the active muscles require up to 3,000 ml. of oxygen per minute–50 times their resting need. Most of this extra oxygen comes from the increased rate and depth of breathing, and it is transported by the increased heart output, but about one-fifth of it comes as a result of blood being shunted away from other organs, such as the spleen (which may be one cause of "stitch"), the liver, the kidneys and the gastro-intestinal tract. Some of the stimulant drugs act by increasing this "shunting" phenomenon. The skin is also involved in the general redistribution, but for a different reason—see below under "body cooling".

'In the first few seconds of exercise, the redistributed blood benefits all the skeletal muscles, whether active or not. Then, very quickly, local metabolites dilate the small arteries and the capillaries in the working muscles, while the blood vessels in the resting muscles constrict.

'The ultimate element of the system of adaptation to exercise, and the beneficiary of the highly adaptable mechanisms for increasing the oxygen supply is, of course, the muscle cell itself. Most of the available energy released by the oxygen is used to interdigitate the filamentous molecular racks inside each muscle cell, thus causing the cell to shorten and, ultimately, the whole muscle to contract. The strength of the contraction depends on how many muscle cells are contracting at any given time, and this in turn depends on how many impulses are passing down the activating or motor nerve to the muscle from the brain.

'One of the ways in which muscle cells are unique is their tolerance to a lack of oxygen. Most other cell types (especially brain cells) are very sensitive to even a short temporary oxygen lack. Muscle cells are able to withstand such hypoxia because of the myoglobin which they contain. As its name suggests, myoglobin is very similar to haemoglobin, both in structure and function. The main difference is that myoglobin does not release its oxygen nearly so easily as haemoglobin—it keeps it until the oxygen lack is more severe. Once the myoglobin has exhausted its oxygen it recharges avidly with oxygen diffusing into the muscle cell (coming from the haemoglobin in the red cells in the capillaries "outside").

'There are two principal energy-releasing pathways in muscle cells. The "main" one (Kreb's citric acid cycle) requires oxygen and glucose as fuel, and forms carbon-dioxide and water as waste products after many stages. The other pathway (anaerobic glycolysis) is only 5 per cent as efficient in extracting energy from glucose, but it can do so *without* oxygen—although with the production of the harmful lactic acid as its waste material.

'Thus the muscle cell has two lines of defence against the relative oxygen lack of intense activity:

1. If the oxygen lack is moderate, then myglobin releases oxygen within the cell to tide it over a short crisis, of a few seconds.

It is the myoglobin recharging-storage mechanism which accounts for the fact that mammalian muscles are most efficient when they are intermittently contracting and relaxing. Brief rest periods, of a few seconds, let the myoglobin recharge–and it is due to myoglobin that the oxygen debt can be accumulated at all.

2. If the oxygen lack is severe, then the muscle cell falls back on its ultimate defence–anaerobic glycolysis–which, as stated, does not require oxygen. However, the end product of glycolysis is lactic acid, which has the penalising disadvantage that increases in its concentration, in muscles and blood, appear to be specifically associated with fatigue. Eventually, fatigue becomes so great that the intensity of the activity must be reduced, or even stopped.

'The lesson from these two groups of facts is that, while an oxygen debt may be acquired every now and then in long rallies throughout a game, lactic acid build-up must be avoided or minimised–or at least kept lower than that of one's opponent. To this end rallies should be kept to a basis of "fair exchange" of effort. (Lactic acid is removed from the blood by the liver and kidneys. In both these organs, though not in muscle, lactic acid is converted back to glucose–the "Cori cycle".)

'A striking illustration of how, by simply varying the periods of intense activity, exactly the same physical task can be made easy, difficult or impossible, is given by the following experiment:

'A trained subject pedalled a bicycle ergometer at a rate which was kept rigidly constant throughout the trial series. If he worked in repetitions of 10 seconds intense activity followed by 20 seconds of rest, then, at the end of 30 minutes of such a regime he felt no subjective fatigue, and his blood lactate (lactic acid) level was 20 mg. per 100 ml., that is, near the resting normal limit.

'If his routine was altered to 30 seconds of work followed by

60 seconds of rest, then at the end of 30 minutes—and having performed exactly the same work, in the same total time as before—the subject felt markedly fatigued and his blood lactate had risen to over 70 mg. per 100 ml.

'Finally, if his routine was altered to 60 seconds work and 120 seconds rest, then he collapsed from complete exhaustion at 24 minutes, with the very high lactate level of 140 mg. per 100 ml.

'In similar experiments with subjects running on a treadmill, 10 seconds of running (at just under five-minute-mile speed) with five second rest period could be maintained for 30 minutes, with moderate fatigue and blood lactate levels in the order of 45 mg. per 100 ml. Similarly, equal proportionate increases in running and rest periods resulted in exhaustion and collapse, with high lactate levels.

'(It is interesting to note that both these types of experiment bear out the old and empirical athletics adage that, "It is not the distance, but the pace, which kills".)

'It has been shown by these and many other similar experiments that, by the introduction of frequent short rests ("micropauses")—which also serve to keep the work periods short—extremely high work loads can be handled aerobically (that is, with minimum recourse to the non-oxygen but lactic acid-forming cycle) without unbearable fatigue.

'The comparison of squash with experiments of this type is natural, because squash is precisely a game of pause and effort, which is the very reason why such a high energy expenditure, or "high workload", can be maintained for over an hour or so. However, the longer the rallies, the greater the danger of forcing the muscles into the lactic acid producing cycle, and the quicker the onset of fatigue. Hence the value of possessing—or developing—a variety of true attacking strokes, with which to terminate unprofitably long rallies, if endurance factors are against one.

'*Body cooling* Another by-product of (both) the muscle energy-releasing cycles is heat. During a hard squash match a man can produce heat at the rate of a one-kilowatt electric fire.

'The reason for the heat production is that, like any machine which performs mechanical work, muscle cannot utilise all the energy in its fuel for work. If one gram of glucose is oxidised in a furnace, 3·9 kcals. are liberated, whereas biological oxidation of one gram of glucose yields 1·5 kcals. as usable energy. Hence the cell is roughly 40 per cent efficient in extracting the energy for work. The remaining 60 per cent of the energy of glucose is released unavoidably as heat and must be dissipated, or severe fever would quickly result.

'During exercise, particularly in a hot climate, the circulation of blood has to fill two competing roles, since part of the heart's output has to be diverted from its primary function of supplying the musculature with nutrients and oxygen to its secondary function of transporting heat to the body surface, that is, to the skin. This sets a limit to the maximum amount of work in hot conditions.

'There are two heat regulating centres in the brain. One promotes heat production in cold conditions, mainly by inducing shivering. The other promotes heat loss, through two groups of nerves. One group controls the calibre of the blood vessels of the skin, the other controls the emptying of the sweat glands. During cold conditions the volume of blood flowing through the skin can fall to as low as one ml. of blood per 100 grams of skin per minute, whereas when one is actively losing heat this blood flow can rise to 100 ml. per 100 grams of skin tissue per minute. (It is due to these skin blood vessels being so dilated that one bruises so easily when hit with the ball.)

'The main components of heat loss are primarily the provision of latent heat for the evaporation of the water secreted as sweat, and, to a lesser extent, the straightforward radiation and convection from the hot skin surface.

'There are approximately two million sweat glands in human skin, and an individual adapted to heat can maintain a sweat rate of a litre an hour for several hours. No other animal can secrete such quantities of fluid with so little loss of other essential body constituents. (It is, of course, mainly due to this high sweat production that one feels thirsty after a game, and also to the large amounts of fluid lost in the breath, as water vapour.)

'It is interesting to note that the lighter, that is, the smaller the person, the better his heat dissipation. This is due to the smaller individual's relatively greater surface area. It is for the same reason that babies are so easily chilled.

'Having studied the components of exercise separately, it is appropriate to consider the whole system together, and then to examine its capabilities for improvement, as occur when an individual becomes physically fit.

'*The prospect of exercise* The very thought of an imminent match can set in motion much physiological preparation. This is experienced as the feeling of nervousness, of "butterflies", before the game. The main preparations are initiated by the (automatic) nervous system, which becomes active and sends impulses to a variety of sites, as a result of which:

The heart rate and its stroke volume both increase.

The respiratory rate increases, and each breath becomes deeper.

The voluntary muscles become tense.

The redistribution of blood begins.

The adrenal glands secrete adrenalin, one's own internal stimulant.

'When the exercise begins, there is an immediate jump in the amount of air breathed, the heart output increases to a maximum in one or two minutes and the haemoglobin starts to release far more of its associated oxygen.

'*Physical fitness* Basically, fitness consists of increasing the efficiency of some of the factors mentioned, as follows:

'*The heart* Regular hard exercise over a period of months increases the size of the heart muscle cells. This "cardiac hypertrophy" enables the heart to increase the force of each beat and to increase its output of blood, compared to the "untrained" heart. A limit to the size of each muscle cell is provided by the fact that as the cell increases in volume, its inner regions become progressively farther from the oxygen diffusing in through the cell surface. Hence there is an optimum size for the cell, beyond which the law of diminishing returns sets in.

'*The muscle cells* (skeletal muscle). With exercise, the volume of the muscles used increases. This, too, is due to an increase in the size of each muscle cell. The increase is mainly due to the formation of new contractile filaments, and also to an increase in the amount of myoglobin in each cell.

'The quantity of myoglobin in the skeletal muscle of an untrained man is about 1·2 mg. per gram of muscle. With training this can be raised to over 7 mg. per gram. The mean total skeletal-muscle myoglobin oxygen store is approximately 250 ml., in untrained subjects (sea level) and averages 1,250 ml. in athletes. In other words, training, by increasing the myoglobin level, provides a bulwark against the glycolysis-lactic acid cycle of energy-with-fatigue.

'There is a possible third mechanism for increasing the muscle workload. It is suggested that constant subjection of muscle cells to the hypoxia of strenuous activity will cause an increase in their content of "respiratory enzymes". These are the chemicals which initiate and catalyse the many stages in the step by step oxidative release of energy from glucose. An increase in the total context or respiratory enzymes per cell would mean that each cell could handle more glucose, produce more energy, and thus perform a greater workload. However, this has been suggested but not proved. (While on the subject, it has recently been established that the mean workload of a random group of Masai men is exceedingly high–on a par with Olympic standards. From this it has been hypothesised that the reason for this remarkable average fitness *might* be that, because of the habitual diet of lactobacillus fermented milk, the Masai may have acquired an unusual tolerance for lactate (perhaps by enzyme induction?), which allows them to persist to higher levels of performance, even with anaerobic metabolism. In other words, the Masai may be able to remove lactic acid from their muscles and blood much faster than "normal". The advantage of this is obvious (however, this has only been theorised, not measured).)

'These factors in muscle cells, the first two of which–the increase in number of contractile filaments and in the amount of myoglobin–are measurably increased with training, combine to give greater power to the muscles involved, as well as an ability for them to work for longer periods without an optimum oxygen supply–while still avoiding lactic acid build-up. This is utilised, for example, when forcing the pace in the final rallies of each game, providing one makes use of the rest periods between games.

'*The circulatory system* The major development here is an increase in the number of the smallest blood vessels, the capillaries, which run between the cells of heart muscle and skeletal muscle. The increase in the muscle-capillary network means that the blood is delivered in even greater quantities, just where it is needed.

'*Haemoglobin* There is probably a small increase in the number of red cells and in the total amount of haemoglobin, following prolonged periods of training (months). However, this is not a major part of physical fitness, except in sportsmen who are acclimatising themselves to altitudes much higher than those to which they are accustomed.

'*The lungs* Following months of severe exercise, there may be some increase in the capacity of the lungs. However, this too is not a major component of fitness under normal conditions.

'Comparatively little work has been done on the effect of cigarette smoking on exercise in relation to the lungs, but smoking is thought to reduce the effectiveness of the lungs to some extent, possibly by constricting the smaller air passages, or by narrowing the lung capillaries, or by increasing the quantity of mucus secreted into the air passages. Probably the effect is a combination of all three.

'*Body weight* Although an indirect factor in fitness, a reduction in body weight often accompanies the process of becoming fit. It is due to a decrease in the amount of body fat.

'All food, whether fat, protein or carbohydrate, once put into the metabolic machinery of the cell can end up as one common denominator, the substance citrate.

'Citrate has a "choice" of two pathways. It can either travel round Kreb's citric acid cycle, releasing energy and ultimately finishing as water and carbon dioxide; *or* citrate may be used as a precursor for synthesising fat. Which way the citrate goes depends on the activity, and hence energy requirements, of the whole organism. Physical exercise sets the citrate on one pathway, inactivity sets it on the other.

'Sixty minutes of hard squash requires an energy expenditure in the order of 900 kcals., which can be supplied in terms of food by a medium sized loaf, or 13 ounces of potatoes, or 12 ounces of lean meat. (Approximately, one ounce of carbohydrate contains 68 kcals., an ounce of protein 76 kcals., and an ounce of fat 162 kcals.) By way of contrast, one ounce of sugar provides enough energy to keep an adult alive for one hour of sleep.

Often, after some weeks of exercise, the decrease in weight is not enough to be felt subjectively – especially as it may amount to a failure to increase, for the main part – but obviously the less weight one has to carry around the court, the better. The one place where a fat loss is felt is when it has been removed from the abdominal wall, because a large pad of abdominal fat, by compressing the organs in the abdominal cavity, may prevent the full excursion of the diaphragm and so prevent the full capacity of the lungs from being used.

'*Heat loss* Thermoregulation is more rapid in people accustomed to frequent hard exercise. They will tend to sweat both earlier and more profusely, and their body temperature and heart rate will not rise as high as persons not in training. Such an increase in efficiency of heat dispersion reaches its useful maximum after a few weeks of hard training.

'Physical fitness is a subject which often provokes heated discussion, mainly because those involved do not accurately define their terms and hence tend to equate different aspects of fitness without realising it.

'In this article I have equated physical fitness with the ability to undergo severe energy expenditure for a relatively long period of time. As this expenditure can be measured, it can be discussed and compared in quantitative terms. High energy expending ability is a firm basis on which to perform many sports. In the specific case of squash, such an ability would certainly embrace "strength and stamina". Naturally, sheer fitness in the energy-expending sense is only part of total preparedness, for any sport.

'As here defined, physical fitness depends on a combination of biochemical and physiological factors, mainly occurring in and around the cells of heart muscle and skeletal muscle. However, the key event in the whole process is the development of the heart.

'Finally, having acquired a reasonable degree of fitness, one must be psychologically capable of using it to the full. This ability depends on the amount of pain one is prepared to tolerate, which in turn depends on one's will to win. As Jonah

Barrington has said of the pain, "It attacks you in the long rallies, but if you're tired and go for winners, winners become losers. I know that if I'm hurt, he's hurt."

'The "pain" is, of course, a consequence of severe oxygen lack, in which context it is of interest to note that it was stated at a recent symposium of the International Union of Biochemistry and Physiological Science, in London, that ". . .regular experience of lack of oxygen as a consequence of muscular activity may be a very effective health factor . . . including the possibility of a better resisting-power to cardio-vascular disease".'

Before moving on to further discussion about fitness it is as well to understand fully what effect diet has on an athlete. Again, this aspect of tennis has been covered in depth in *Lawn Tennis* magazine, which published, in September 1967, an important article by Dr. R. V. Qureshi of the Biochemistry Unit of Glaxo Research:

'The success of a tennis player not only depends upon his knowledge of the game and how accurately he can place his returns in the opponent's court but also on the number of sets he can play with the same speed and excellence without suffering strain. His quick reactions and sound judgement are as vital to him as his physical fitness. All this he learns on a tennis court by improving his performance through hard training which, in addition to giving him mastery of the game, builds his stamina, which is extremely important whether he plays Club or Tournament Tennis.

'The degree of physical fitness of a player depends upon his health and the state of his nutrition. A good diet balanced with respect to its nutrients affords better health. It would be a hard task, and probably unfair, to compose a diet for a tennis player and generalise it as a panacea for best results. A good diet is mainly composed of proteins, fats, carbohydrates, minerals and vitamins. These five constituents are present in most of our customary dishes and a complete meal is derived from the choice of these dishes. An average British diet provides about 76·5 g (2·6 oz.) of protein, 118 g (4·2 oz.) of fat and 343 g. (12 oz.) of carbohydrate per day. It is a matter of common knowledge that the food we eat is metabolised in our bodies to keep us warm, maintain our body weight, support growth and meet with the daily demands of wear and tear of our tissues. All these functions can be expressed in terms of energy utilisation which can be calculated from the amount and type of food eaten and measured as calories of heat. In these terms our average British diet gives a total of 2,650 calories per person per day, of which carbohydrates contribute about 48 per cent, fat about 40 per cent, and proteins about 11 per cent. In such a diet the chief source of calories would be carbohydrate in all its forms, such as, hams, sweets, cakes, biscuits and puddings; potatoes and bread. Proteins come largely from all kinds of meat, fish, eggs, bread, milk and cheese. The main sources of fat are margarine, butter, cooking oils, dairy products and meat.

'From the nutritional point of view carbohydrates are regarded as energy-yielding foods, each gram of which equals roughly 4 calories. Fats are a concentrated form of energy, giving about 9 calories per gram. Proteins are important as body-building constituents in our food, but if used for energy each gram of protein provides about 4 calories. In a mixed diet, such as the British diet, minerals like calcium and iron, and vitamins, for example A, D, B1, B2 and C are present in ample amounts to meet the ordinary requirements of most individuals.

'An average British diet is adequate for an average British person, but in practice averages seldom exist. People do not look alike, grow alike or eat alike. Dietary requirements of one group of the population differ from those of other groups of the population; for example, men require more food than women. The dietary requirements within a group also vary considerably, for instance, two tennis players playing the same number of sets a day may have widely differing dietary requirements. There are certain well defined criteria from which it is possible to obtain a good idea of one's caloric and protein requirements. People normally eat enough to satisfy their appetites which are sated if enough calories are consumed. It is of course possible to satisfy appetite without consuming the required protein, vitamin and mineral needs, but if, as is usually the situation in countries such as our own, a varied diet is consumed, the mixture of foods so provided will amply supply the body's needs for all the varied nutrients. A diet of steaks and beer alone would be as bad as one of potatoes and cream cakes; fortunately most people find such diets monotonous, and given the chance, will eat a variety of foods so that in the mixture eaten during the course of the day all the nutrients needed may be met even though none of the foods consumed would, by themselves, supply all the components essential for life and health.

'The energy requirements of individuals are dependent upon physical activity, body size, age and climatic environment. In Great Britain young men between the ages of 20 and 30 years, weighing 65 kilograms (144 lbs.), employed daily in 8 hours of non-sedentary work and about 3 hours of sporting activities, require 3,200 calories per day. Young women similarly employed, weighing 55 kilograms (121 lbs.), and having about 2 hours of sporting activities, require 2,300 calories. These men and women will require 2,750 and 2,250 calories if sporting activities are substituted by light work. By the age of 50 years, the requirements will have fallen by about 5 per cent and by a further 5 to 10 per cent in the following decade.

'The energy requirements (E) of people with different body weights (W) (in kilograms) can be calculated by using the following simple equations:

$$\text{For men:} \quad E = 815 + 36 \cdot 6W$$
$$\text{For women:} \quad E = 58 + 31 \cdot 1W$$
$$(1 \text{ kilogram} = 2 \cdot 2 \text{ lb.})$$

'The energy expenditure in different kinds of activities varies quite considerably. At rest it ranges from 0·7 to 1·2 cals./minute. In light work, such as playing bowls or cooking, it is between 2·5 and 5 cals./minute, and in moderate work, such as cycling or scrubbing floors about 5 to 7 cals./minute; heavy work utilizes 7–10 cals./minute.

'A good tennis player is assumed to expend between 6 and 9 cals./minute depending on whether he plays singles or doubles. His energy expenditure for one set lasting for half an hour would be between 180 and 270 calories. In four sets he would expend between 700 and 1,000 calories. Subtracting the calories which he would have expended in very light work instead of playing tennis, his caloric requirements would thus increase by about 500 to 700 calories.

143

'In Britain and the other affluent countries, proteins in the diet come from various sources. In our average national consumption of proteins, about 60 per cent are derived from animal sources, such as milk, eggs, fish and meat, and the rest come from vegetable sources, largely wheat and potatoes. As a rule, the utilization and thus quality of animal proteins and proteins from mixed sources is higher than proteins from vegetable sources. Where the concentration of proteins in a diet is much higher than the requirements, the excess proteins are utilized as energy just like that from carbohydrates. The proteins are more expensive than the carbohydrates, therefore excessive amount of proteins in a diet is not good value for money. On the other hand, if the concentration of proteins in a diet is low, functions such as growth, body building and repair of the tissues are impaired.

'An average adult male requires 1·4 grams and an average adult female requires 1·3 grams of mixed proteins per kilogram of body weight. Protein requirements expressed as grams per day for average sized man and woman would be about 90 grams (3·2 oz.) and 72 grams (2·5 oz.) respectively. Taking protein and calory requirements into account, the concentration of mixed proteins in a diet should range from 10 to 12·5 per cent. The average British diet contains 11·0 per cent proteins and is, therefore, quite adequate from the point of view of protein requirements.

'An individual capable of maintaining his body weight on 2,500 calories per day would presumably require 700 additional calories after playing four sets of tennis. He could meet the extra demand for calories in many ways: he could, for instance, eat either 3 oz. of butter or 6¼ oz. of sugar or 4 oz. of sweet biscuits or 10 oz. of white bread or potato chips, or 7½ oz. of mixed fruit pudding. He could also derive the same number of calories from either 37 oz. of fresh whole milk or about 6 oz. of Cheddar cheese or 10 oz. of fried eggs or 8 oz. of grilled beef steak or 7½ oz. of fried pork sausages or 12 oz. of fried cod. He could also obtain 700 calories by drinking 78 oz. of bitter draught ale.

'There are a few guiding principles which would help him in the choice of food. Fortunately, he does not need to eat the equivalent of an additional 700 calories in one of his usual meals, because such a large meal many people would at first find difficult to consume. The man in need of extra energy can increase the amount of food eaten at each meal and so spread the extra consumption throughout the day. He could eat extra snacks, an extra full meal at some convenient time during the day or substitute a full meal for the morning or afternoon cup of tea. For many people this is not convenient so extra energy-rich drinks, which are easy to make and quickly swallowed are often employed. For this purpose pure sugar or glucose can be used, but if so it should be remembered that these do not provide any nutrients, apart from energy, and if taken in the required amount may lead to temporary stomach discomfort. On the other hand sugars are said to be useful in that they are very quickly absorbed and utilised. There are proprietary mixtures, which are more pleasant to taste, which do provide extra nutrients and can be consumed as drinks to give rapidly assimilable energy.

'Body water constitutes approximately two-thirds of the body weight. A man weighing 65 kilograms (144 lb.) would contain about 40 litres (9 gallons) of water. The maintenance of water balance in the body is as important a criterion as any other for good health. In addition to the water output from the kidneys an appreciable volume of water is lost from the skin by sweating. The latter loss can be considerable during strenuous exercise. A tennis player on a hot summer day might lose between 3 and 5 litres ($\frac{3}{4}$ and 1 gallon) of his body water through sweating and unless this water is replaced by an increased intake, the body will become dehydrated. Severe symptoms have been reported as a result of a loss of about 10 per cent of total body water. The volume of water in the body is controlled by the amount of fluid drunk which in turn depends on thirst.

'Amongst other water soluble substances which are excreted through the skin, sodium chloride (common salt) is of significance. Under conditions of excessive sweating correspondingly large quantities of salt can be lost from the body. Lack of salt can lead to muscular cramp. The requirement of common salt would therefore be larger.

145

'To summarise, one would suggest that a player should enjoy a varied diet, use his appetite and thirst as a guide to the amount to eat, and so take extra snacks or drinks as needed. He should make sure that he does take some salt and normally he will find it more comfortable and convenient to satisfy his appetite by frequent snacks or energy-rich but readily digestible foods rather than by a few heavy meals.'

There are a few practical points to be added, arising from a lecture given by Donald L. Cooper, M.D., at the American Health Association's 43rd Annual Conference.

He emphasised that the heavy protein (meat dominated) diet came into vogue in Greece around 500 B.C. and was based on a theory that, since 'muscle' was so important in strenuous exercise, athletes might perform better if they replenished muscle by eating more muscle, or meat. When meat diets proved successful, the coaches put two and two together but made the answer five. The meat predominating diet still flourishes but the need for a sound balance of proteins, carbohydrates and fats is gaining wider recognition.

Particularly before play proteins should actually be avoided. Digestion and metabolism of protein leaves a residue of acid in muscle and this can only be cleared by the kidneys. But the kidneys cease to be effective during exercise so anyone eating meat, eggs or other protein food less than three hours before an important match is exposing himself to the risk of cramps, acidosis and fatigue.

Further, carbohydrates are 10 per cent more efficient than proteins or fats in utilising oxygen and oxygen utilisation governs the rate at which lactic acid is dispersed from the muscles.

In selecting a pre-game diet, the main consideration is to avoid foods that will impede the athlete. Dr. Cooper doubted that a special diet can enhance performance, but serious impairments can be avoided: loose bowels, abdominal cramps, delayed emptying of the stomach, depleted salt stores and inadequate energy supplies.

The important pre-game period for endurance events begins about 48 hours before the event (for short-term events, diet at this time will modify performance little if at all). Irritating or 'gassy' foods, roughage and other foods which increase stool bulk should now be eliminated. Salads, spices, oils and alcohol should be omitted, as well as fats, which slow the normal emptying time of the stomach. Otherwise, the diet should not be drastically altered, except for the final pre-event meal which is eaten three or more hours before the contest.

This meal must be highly digestible, as normal digestive processes may be altered in the keyed-up athlete. 'Much of the traditional pre-game meal never gets out of the stomach, so it cannot do anything but harm,' said Dr. Cooper.

One of the well-balanced liquid formulae on the market may help to avoid this problem. Other foods which are acceptable are toast with honey, oatmeal, weak tea or coffee with sugar, and peaches in heavy syrup.

Bouillon cubes are a good source of salt if sweating is a problem. Salt tablets may be taken with the pre-game meal but not just before the contest, when they may cause vomiting.

As for vitamins, Dr. Cooper believed that while b-complex vitamins might be of some value, their effect on athletic performance is probably a perfectly acceptable psychological one.

Since the end of 1969 the value of a 'natural' diet has been recognised by a number of players, of whom Mark Cox is the most notable. This is too specialised and complex to be covered here but those interested should read *Folk Medicine*.[1]

Simultaneously, the value of the preparation Bio-Strath has come into prominence and this deserves examination. Once again, the extent of your advancement is geared to marginal factors. The more you progress, the more you need to take these factors into account. Each one may only be worth one point in an entire match but twelve such factors add up to three whole games and that is considerable.

There is one other general aspect to be understood and that is sleep. This was dealt with thoroughly by Francis Thorne in *Lawn Tennis* some years ago. He wrote:

'We spend a third of our lives asleep, yet although much is known about the physical changes connected with this phenomenon, the sleep mechanism and the mental changes associated

[1] By D. C. Jarvis, M.D. (Pan Books).

with it remain a mystery–Nature has kept this secret closely guarded. Nevertheless, some useful facts have been gleaned, so let us examine what is known about sleep.

'Sleep is a state of unconsciousness occurring at regular periods during which the body, especially the nervous system, is refreshed and rejuvenated. It is the most complete form of rest because most of the body organs take time off during sleep; only the digestive, breathing and circulatory systems continue to work, and these only at a reduced rate, and therefore relaxation is more or less complete.

'When sleep comes upon one, sight and smell are the first senses to be lost; hearing and touch go more slowly–a loud noise or a push will waken most people. The faculty first affected is will-power–and it is the last to return–hence the difficulty in getting up when the alarm clock bids! Leaping straight out of bed is not a good thing anyway. It is better to muse for a bit and rise slowly, thereby allowing the blood pressure to return to normal without strain. Reasoning and the association of ideas go after will-power–then memory and imagination.

'On the physical plane blood pressure drops, we generate less heat and energy, body-temperature falls (and the blood supply to the brain becomes feeble), respiration is slower and deeper, the heart beats slower, the kidneys produce less urine, and the liver less bile. The skin becomes flushed with blood, hence the need to have enough covering, to avoid chills.

'Contrary to the general belief, the deepest period of sleep is the first one to two hours, after which sleep grows lighter to just below the threshold of consciousness, until the fourth to fifth hour, when we once more relapse into deep sleep and relaxation for a while before progressing by stages to wakefulness.

'There are many theories about the cause of sleep. One is that the nervous impulses from the brain are blocked, another postulates the idea of a toxin (a poison) being responsible through accumulating during the waking hours until it permeates and dulls the central nervous system. Then there is the idea that an acid–a waste product of energy–clogs the nervous system in a similar way. Yet another is that toward the end of the day, especially after strenuous mental or physical exertion, our body cells and brain become deprived of oxygen, thus producing sleep. In fact, of the oxygen taken in over 24 hours, 67 per cent is taken in during the 12 hours of day, and 33 per cent during the 12 hours of night, so there may be something in this theory. The latest idea is that inhibition, always present in the brain, spreads over the body during sleep rather like night ousting day in the sky. The act of going to bed and all the preliminaries connected therewith condition the brain for sleep and aid the inhibitory process. Tenable as some of these ideas seem, they are but theories–the exact mechanism of sleep remains a mystery.

'How much sleep we need depends on occupation, age and perhaps on sex, although the authorities seem to differ on whether men need more sleep than women. Some people can get by on a succession of "cat naps" some need only a few hours daily, others are "whacked" without eight to ten hours. There are, of course, individual variations, and habit plays its part. It can be said, however, that brain workers need more sleep than those engaged in manual labour, and the young certainly need more than the old. A child of four requires about thirteen hours, young children about twelve hours and until fifteen ten hours, thereafter reducing until eight hours at nineteen. As a general rule, for adults the average of eight hours holds good. Old people need less.

'If you lose much sleep you will soon show signs of it. Prolonged deprivation of sleep will reduce a man to a parlous state. The usual symptoms are lack of concentration, irritability and fatigue. The eyes become heavy-lidded and sore, and there may be loss of appetite. These symptoms cause anxiety which in turn affects sleep and so the vicious circle goes on until broken by treatment.

'It has been stated that the loss of one night's sleep can be detected for a week. On the other hand, it is reported that a man who stayed awake for 230 hours (under drugs) was fresh again after only 11 hours sleep. An experiment conducted to see how long people could stay awake voluntarily showed 115 hours as the highest reading. Generally, Nature sees that sleep intervenes before any permanent harm is done, and most sleep deficits are made up during one good night's sleep. This leads to the question of insomnia.

'Highly strung and emotional people are more prone to sleeplessness than the placid types and the commonest causes are idleness during the day, mental stimulation at night, excitement and a fear of insomnia. A hot drink, and/or a warm bath before retiring, light reading in bed, a combination of these will often induce sleep, but where the condition is obstinate a doctor should be consulted.

'A little planning in the bedroom can do much to lessen the chance of sleepless nights.

'There must be adequate ventilation. During the day leave the windows open to clear away "bedroom fug"; at night leave one window open at least. Add another blanket to the bed rather than close the window. Do not, however, overload the bed with blankets. This is a common cause of restless sleep. A hard mattress is preferable to a soft one; most interior sprung mattresses of modern design are quite suitable, but avoid the feather bed like the plague. This encourages defects in posture. See that the bed is placed away from draughts and that the reading lamp gives a good light, and is in a convenient position. Craning the neck to catch the light won't help to induce sleep. Quiet is essential, but some people find a mild rhythmic noise, like the tick of a clock, soothing.

'Perhaps the most important thing is to establish a sleep rhythm. This means adhering to a set routine. Prepare for, and go to bed at the same time each night. This conditions the mind and body for sleep and establishes the rhythm; late nights break it.

'Don't attempt mental gymnastics before retiring, nor engage in heated discussion.

'The best guarantee of sound sleep is a pleasantly tired body and a quiet mind.'

The psychological value of sufficient sleep and moderation – abstinence even – in activities like drinking, smoking and the opposite sex cannot easily be measured.

If you have the right philosophical attitude you will accept that the most you can hope for on court is to play the very best tennis of which you are capable. You will use every scrap of your mental and physical resolution and skill in trying for victory, accepting that if you achieve this yet still lose, you must intensify the quality and quantity of your practice and training to become a better player.

This attitude is highly dependent on an untroubled mind and this you can only have at four games all in the final set if you have trained for many weeks to the limits of your abilities. This is not the time to be diverted by tiredness and a regret that you had not gone straight home after the cinema instead of going for a coffee and socialising with an affectionate partner.

At four-all in the final set you need to call up every scrap of effort within your capabilities and not to be hindered by stray doubts about your lack of long-term training. Peace of mind has a value beyond academic understanding.

You are likely to hear the word 'staleness' from time to time, perhaps even to believe you have played too much; that you are stale and in need of a rest. It could be true—but it is unlikely. Unquestionably there is a limit to the amount of nerve strain a man can tolerate without rest. This was first emphasised by Lord Moran during World War I in his classic book *The Anatomy of Courage* and widely recognised by the R.A.F. during World War II when they maintained extensive records of bomber crew behaviour, reaction and psychic disorders. These revealed that after a short rise in performance and morale during the early missions there was a gradual tailing away which manifested itself in loss of body weight, sleeplessness and an increase in psychic disorders. Performance and morale suffered and in some cases it was necessary to take men off operations. There was one cure—rest.

Now while no one in his right senses would attempt to compare the stresses of even a Davis Cup Challenge Round with those of a bombing mission over the Ruhr, competitive tennis is stressful.

Staleness shows itself in lethargy, lack of interest, tiredness and no ability to win. Other signs are abnormal anxiety about the chances of winning, increasing irritability and decreasing tolerance of frustration, even in small matters, complaints about minor ailments and gradual loss of weight.

Personally, the idea of rest lacks appeal. My attitude to improvement is always positive. So if you really do become stale–and you will not if you are really dedicated–change your training schedule. Particularly, ensure that practice and training are pleasurable. There is a puritanical goodness which steals over many people after a strenuous, well conducted training session. If that session has been enjoyable–and training can be enjoyable–the change will have been right and all further thoughts of staleness can safely be dismissed.

12 · What to Aim at in Training

Back in 1948 Bob Falkenberg precipitated hundreds of column inches of hostile newspaper reporting because of the immense amount of time he spent prone on the court after falls. He threw many sets, some of them 6–0. Years later it was discovered that he had a thyroid deficiency and it was a wonder that he could play one competitive set, let alone the five he needed to save three match points and beat John Bromwich in the Wimbledon final. His stamina was bedrock minimal but he still became champion.

His is an extreme case and one which in no sense should be repeated through failure to develop stamina. Yet it does reinforce my contention, based on forty-two years of playing, writing and watching, that the single most important physical asset is speed. That is, speed of thought, reaction and movement, especially over the first two yards.

Careful watching of your ball and your opponent's develops insight into habits and techniques, so improving that other valuable asset, anticipation. This is essential because even sheer speed is insufficient in top class tennis where 100 m.p.h. services and 80 m.p.h. volleys are common. At that speed you have less than half a second to return service and around a quarter of a second between many volleys and responding passing shots. There is no place for sluggards at this speed.

Speed is the product of two main factors: muscle 'explosiveness' and power-to-weight ratio. Whatever innate strength you possess has to overcome basic body inertia. The lighter the body, the less inertia to overcome. So for an athlete as much as for a racing car, the aim must be constantly to increase the power-to-weight ratio. This is largely a question of brute strength, but not of bulky, inelastic muscles. Flexibility and power must be improved in tandem.

Today, weight training is generally considered to be the best method of developing power. However, a number of misconceptions about weight training persist. The following article dispels some of them; it was written by Al Murray for *Lawn Tennis*. Mr. Murray, an Olympic coach, is the man behind the gold medals of Mary Rand and Louis Martin. He knows his subject inside out and is always developing techniques.

'Tennis is a tough, red-blooded, power game, but I doubt if there are many players who really understand just how much power is required to reach a high competitive standard.

'Naturally, it must be understood that there are many qualities of equal importance to power; such attributes as skill, speed, stamina, quick reaction, determination, etc., and these are more fully understood and appreciated than the quality of power.

'Power in simple engineering terms is Force times Velocity, and to put real power into your tennis you must apply these principles.

'Therefore, your training must consist of a reasonable amount of time spent on the development of strength which is the essence of power. Raw strength is best understood as the ability to overcome resistance without the assistance of speed or technique. Simple examples of raw strength are as follows:

'The bending of an iron bar across one knee; uprooting a young tree; trying to undo a stuck screw-top lid; lifting a weight that is so heavy that it just clears the floor.

'However, if the weight is not near one's limit, skill and speed are then included, and this movement then becomes *one of power*.

'So if power is to be increased, strength, speed and technique must be improved. However, it is usually the quality of strength which is well below par, neglected and not clearly understood. There is no quicker and better method of strength and power building than by the correct application of progressive weight training.

'The advantages of weight training are simple to appreciate:

  (a) The correct resistance can be selected to suit age, sex and physical condition.
  (b) The weight can be gently progressed, even by half a pound as the exerciser's power is increased.
  (c) The weight can be quickly adjusted to suit the strength and size of the muscle group to be exercised.

(d) The exercising position can be altered so that the resistance can be thrown on any specific section of a particular tennis movement.

(e) By altering the number of repetitions, or groups of repetitions, or the weight, one can alter the effects of the weight-training schedule. Several groups of very low repetitions with heavy weights will build strength and power, where on the other hand one or two groups of very high fast repetitions, with light weights and short rests between each group develop stamina and cardiovascular efficiency.

'Between those two extremes of method lie a wide variety of obtainable results, mainly in the balance and proportion of these three qualities: power, stamina, mobility.

'What results can be obtained from weight training? Naturally, if our main interest is tennis, we should not waste time and energy on non-result-producing items of training. Therefore, it is necessary to analyse the situation and especially the anticipated rewards for our efforts.

'By exercising against resistances which can be easily graded you can quickly build strength and power in the muscle or muscle group involved in any one particular tennis stroke or movement. Additional power in the legs and hip will enable you to transport your body weight in a fast explosive manner, hit harder when required, and greatly help to eliminate or cut down minor muscular and joint injuries. Above all, weight training is the most condensed form of training possible and one half-hour session twice or three times weekly can produce fantastic results.

'This is why people like Mary Rand spend time on weight training. Despite her feminine attractiveness she has progressed to the stage where she uses really heavy weights but the resistance is still relative to her sex, physical condition, and requirements for her particular events.

'Weight training no doubt still brings to many minds someone struggling with a great load. This is utter rubbish. If you sit at your desk wagging your pencil you are doing a very elementary form of weight training and progress from there on is simply a case of adding gently to the resistance. Increases should be governed by your age, sex and physical condition and not the condition or ability of the man next door.

'Suitable weight-training outfits for tennis power building are not expensive, and have the advantage of no depreciation in value.'

The really serious and ambitious player can measure progress in strength to weight ratio, though he may have to visit a gymnasium or coach to do so.

It is necessary to have access to grip, leg and back dynamometers for they measure strength in pounds of force. The gripping strength of the right and left hands, the strength of the legs together and then the back strength–these figures added together should, in the case of a top class tennis player, be from 16 to 18 times his body weight.

Possibly no activity demands greater muscular explosive power than shot-putting. Recent champion Arthur Rowe had the ideal proportions: 200 lbs. right hand, 600 lbs. back strength, 1,800 lbs. legs strength–a ratio of one, three, nine. He was a big man. He could run 100 yards in 10·2 seconds although he was not a serious sprinter. His 9·2 seconds for a 50 yards shuttle run was the finest in the country a decade ago.

Let me make it clear that strength and power are not synonymous. Strength measures how much mass you can move. Power is the rate at which you can do it–and that is the key factor in tennis.

Muscular speed is difficult to improve. This demands strength, good running or stroking technique and muscular relaxation. Muscular relaxation is a facet of training which has been neglected, perhaps because it is not yet well understood.

Experts like Graham Adamson of Leeds University–he is fitness consultant to Leeds United F.C.–have noticed the tremendous, frightening power developed by madmen, men having fits and men struggling for their lives. Untrained they may be but with all inhibitions released, their power multiplies staggeringly. But were they ever intended to unleash such power? Are the inhibitions nature's protection against self-inflicted damage? These are questions not yet fully understood or answered.

Meanwhile, watching a pianist like Rubinstein playing at

speed, one notices the complete relaxation of his fingers. Without it he could never achieve such rapid fingering.

Sound, well grooved physical movements and strokes undoubtedly make for muscular efficiency and that, in turn, breeds confidence. Confidence is an antidote to tension and nervousness. Tension and nervousness utterly oppose relaxation. So when you suffer either, make a conscious effort to relax.

For building stamina, there is nothing to compare with interval running. This is the finest way to acquire endurance of heart and lungs. Running round tracks or roads is not everyone's idea of heaven but there is no real substitute. If three or four men join forces and make it into some kind of a game, it helps. But a champion-to-be is blessed with the mental drive to do it alone. It was such mental drive that converted Jonah Barrington from a squash rackets nonentity into the world's best player in the space of two years. At the end of that second year we discussed his views on training and the following is extracted from what appeared in *Lawn Tennis*:

BARRINGTON: The pain barrier is just about the most important thing in the game. It is a mental barrier which very few people seem to be able to break through at the highest class. It means that one has got to build up in training enough willpower and determination so that in a match one will be able to sustain punishment. To feel really on one's last legs and yet recover and fight and play a consistent ball instead of going for an easy winner.

What normally happens is that a player gets tired and when he gets tired he looks for the easy way to end rallies and then he makes errors. The top-class player who can meet the pain barrier will, when he is tired, play himself back in the match by hoisting high balls, deliberately conserving himself by playing a safer game but having control over himself. It is this mental control when feeling hurt that so few people have.

I think one can only build up this mental control by really assiduous practice in training. In other words one has got to hurt oneself skipping, running, and so on. Whatever exercises one is doing one has got to hurt oneself and then one can brave this barrier in these matches.

What to Aim at in Training

You say 'hurt'. Is this the hurt of the wind or the muscles or the mind or all?

BARRINGTON: In the main it is the hurt of the wind. The hurt that comes in the stomach and in the chest. But if one is doing weight-training one has got to hurt the muscles. One must work oneself so that one tires. One must not always play within oneself, lift weights that are comfortable but instead push for that little extra poundage and take that heavier bit of punishment.

It is very difficult to do this day after day after day, yet it is vital to form a habit of doing so frequently. Then in the game the barrier does not seem so big as it would otherwise. In fact it is virtually impossible for people who do not undertake this extra work off court to overcome the pain barrier.

When Roger Bannister ran the first four-minute mile he drove himself into a very bad oxygen debt and very nearly collapsed simply through lack of oxygen. Have you in training tried to take yourself into those extreme conditions of punishment?

BARRINGTON: What I attempt to do in training is to hurt myself, if I am running, rather on the lines of interval training— to hurt myself and rest; I am not pushing myself to the limit. Even in my training runs I am doing a form of interval training in that I am hurting myself every now and then but not pushing myself to the limit.

What I attempt is to put in a sustained burst, a crippling burst for maybe 800 yards, maybe longer than that, knowing what the final goal is, and to force myself over that period.

The pain is gradually building up and over the last 600 yards the feeling one has is 'My God, I wish this would stop!' But forcing oneself to go those extra yards, knowing that this is the sort of pain one may feel in the fifth game of a top squash match and imagining that this is an opponent who must be defeated, forcing oneself because of these factors is the key which opens the door to advancement.

Have you done any measurement of actual speed over distances?

BARRINGTON: It would be very interesting. Some friends, some of the squash players, think that I would run a very fast half-mile, and others think that I would run a particularly fast 10 miles! I haven't done anything like that as yet.

What to Aim at in Training

In your semi-final against Ken Hiscoe you lost 7 lb. in weight and against Dick Carter you lost almost 8 lb. How much pain did that cause you on the court?

BARRINGTON: I must have hit my barrier about four times in the final; and in the semi-final it would probably have been about the same. In the final I particularly remember the second game. Even though I had not done very much work in the first game, in the second game (it was perhaps largely mental) I felt the game wasn't going very well and that I was tiring. This was an easy barrier to get over as soon as I had won a couple of points. But later on in the match there were occasions when he seemed to be in better condition than me but I managed to master this mental thing in time.

In fact I was never, probably, as tired as I thought. One does have the feeling that there must be some reason for feeling tired and it came into my head that perhaps I hadn't recovered fully from Saturday's battle, but I don't think that was so at all.

Did you at any time concede any single point against Carter or against Hiscoe out of tiredness, mental tiredness, or try for a winner too soon in the rally?

BARRINGTON: Yes, in the fourth game against Carter, when I needed to play very tightly, he was either 5–4 or 6–4 and he pushed a high ball, a volley, a half–lob, across court fairly deep.

I tried to volley it short on my backhand and planted it firmly into the middle of the tin. As I played that shot I knew I was letting myself down, giving in to a feeling of tiredness – that I couldn't really go on and that I must go for my winners early. This is what we were talking about earlier. In fact I should have played a high volley down the wall. It wasn't bravery that made me try for a winner, I was doing it out of cowardice really.

That was the one point that I gave away through the feeling that I was too tired to play out a long rally. But the extraordinary thing is that about two minutes later I was back in hand at 4–7 and I was feeling almost elated at this stage because I felt that at last I was at grips. I knew that he would be feeling rather apprehensive having reached 7 because it is just that little bit too far away from point for the match and I felt that he would be rather tense at that stage and might well make errors.

What to Aim at in Training

Before that he had been waiting for my errors and so I did my best and as it was a tricky situation played a very, very tight five points. In fact, the errors then came from him and I think I won 14 points in a row. From 4–7 down I went to game and then 9–0 in the fifth game in one hand. It was quite fantastic that at 4–6 or 4–5 I put a volley in to the tin out of tiredness and inability to discipline myself and then suddenly I disciplined myself entirely as if I was infuriated by what I had done. Disciplined myself as I had not done before and played much better than at any other time of the match.

The importance of good lungs and heart cannot be over-emphasised. When we exercise, lactic acid builds up in the muscles, so tiring them. Oxygen inhibits the excess production of this acid, so postponing the onset of fatigue and allowing the muscles to go on working. Oxygen is taken in by the lungs and pumped in blood to the muscles by the actions of the heart. So a fit athlete must develop a good oxygen up-take and a long, slow, powerful heart beat.

Interval running does just this. Allied to weight training, shuttle running and circuit training, it will slowly and inexorably improve lung efficiency and bring your pulse rate down from 70 or so to 60, 50, 40, 30 or even lower.

Agility and turning–bending efficiency is of great importance. Fast skipping aids speed but potato races are better. Put a bucket down on the court, scatter a dozen potatoes at distances varying from two to five yards from the bucket and then see how quickly you can get the potatoes into that bucket. It is a killing exercise but very effective.

Françoise Durr, perhaps the most nimble woman in tennis, has her own variation of this. She goes on court with a racket and then chases all over the place after imaginary balls hit by a non-existent opponent. Remember, though, that transference effects in training are slight. Potato races primarily make you better at potato races, skipping at skipping, so always ally training and court practice–and without too long intervals.

Follow your potato races with a spell of 'threesomes': that is, have two men at the other end of the court firing tennis balls at you as fast as they can. As soon as one goes out of play another is immediately hit. They should chase you up and down and from side to side with sadistic speed and without respite. That is the way to develop all the speeds—of racket, movement, reaction, mobility, agility—at the same time and so gain co-ordination and effectiveness under conditions simulating top-class match play.

As you progress you will seek help from other people and devise your own schedules. Right away, take an honest look at your physical composition and decide what is needed. Certainly run the roads three or four nights a week, perhaps in heavy boots, though I am not entirely convinced of the extra benefit of this.

Undertake circuit training—the L.T.A. circuit is appended, appendix A—but try to keep training fun. Without in any way encouraging laziness, I think training during a genuine period of staleness is, at best, of no benefit and at worst harmful.

But when are you stale? Not as often as you think and never when you are winning. When you are losing it is easy to let go mentally for a while, to make excuses, to believe you are tired.

This is when the men are sorted out from the boys. That is when you should follow the example of Jonah Barrington when he was beaten in the first world squash championships and his world fell about him.

His friends advised a one evening break from his monkish existence and went to organise a sympathetic companion while Jonah moved towards the shower. When the friends returned and looked in the shower, they did not at first see Jonah. Then they looked down. There was Jonah doing some press-ups, having decided that there was only one course open: learn from the defeat and become a fitter, better player for the next time.

Such is the thinking and the spirit of champions.

Perhaps belatedly in this book, I must condemn gamesmanship, which is a polite word for cheating or near cheating.

It would be foolish in this materialistic age to deny that cheating is sometimes financially beneficial, mainly in the short run. The really great champions—Laver, Newcombe, Rosewall, Roche, Gonzales, Margaret Court—are far too immense in spirit ever to demean themselves by stooping to such methods.

What to Aim at in Training

As much as they have developed their techniques and tactics, so have they increased the bigness of their personalities. It would be stupid to assert that none of them has ever transgressed, for all are human. Yet all, through instinct or design, have been far too much concerned with the vital aspects of their advancement ever to concern themselves with petty methods which must, in the end, lessen them as people and, therefore, as players.

Granted that gamesmanship may occasionally bring short term rewards, in the long term it diverts from the all-demanding necessity of using every ounce of ingenuity in improving and so attaining the ranks of the 'giants'. And giants eventually gain more in money, prestige and affection than petty traffickers in the dubious fields of near cheating. So if you have any self-respect, never stoop to unfair practices. Instead, commit yourself utterly to winning. Let that completely override all other considerations. Your opponent has three net cords and two doubtful line calls in a space of minutes. The dedicated winner – the champion – may explode momentarily; but by the start of the next point will have pushed all this out of his mind and again be entirely directed to winning.

He will never, like so many non-champions, devote only ninety per cent of his effort to winning, spending the other ten per cent on, say, repeated glances at the linesman or umpire, in the hope of establishing an 'alibi' if he loses – 'of course, I would have won, but . . .?'

That form of alibi-establishment is all too apparent. Others may be less so but they are equally culpable. It needs honesty and courage to shun them all, especially those which excuse defeat to oneself, because then any subsequent losses have nothing to cushion them. They hurt – badly. But they also teach how to use misfortune itself to climb higher, and ultimately to achieve one's full potential, which normally proves infinitely greater than one believed it to be.

So shed ruthlessly all false pride, self-delusion, and irrelevant appearances. Commit yourself unreservedly to overcoming your opponent and your weaknesses. Be true to yourself at all times and you will enjoy the peace and satisfaction which follows the complete giving of one's best.

Appendix A

TRAINING FOR LAWN TENNIS

The following programme is designed to give the player a basic physical fitness without which he cannot attain his full potential as a player, regardless of the amount of talent he has. It is not a substitute for playing practice on the court and is complementary to learning the skills of the game.

Remember that it is better to do physical training 'a little and often' rather than to train for long periods at irregular intervals. The first method can be enjoyed, the second tends to discourage further efforts. The following exercises are designed to increase your speed, strength and stamina – the three basic requirements of physical fitness. They require a minimum of equipment and need no special skill to perform.

THE EXERCISES

(1) *Bench Steps.* Step on to a bench (low enough to reach without undue effort) and off again. Legs must be straightened when on the bench. Lead with left leg for half number repetitions. Right leg for other half.

(2) *Trunk Curls* (lying). Flat on back with hands clasped behind head. Keeping legs straight bend up to touch knees with forehead.

(3) *Press-Ups.* Front support position on finger-tips. Keeping the whole body straight bend and straighten arms.

(4) *Chest Raising.* Lying face downwards with hands clasped behind back, arms straight. Lift head, shoulders and chest off floor.

(5) *Toe Touching.* Stand with legs apart. Keeping legs straight, touch the ground outside feet, in front of you and through legs then back to vertical.

163

(6) *Double Knee Jumps.* Stand on toes, with feet together. Leap up and bound knees against chest and back to starting position.

(7) *Chin Heave.* Stand beneath a bar that you can just grip with arms straight. Pull up until chin is level with bar, then lower and bounding off the ground between heaves.

(8) *Vertical Punch.* Holding dumb-bell (or a brick) in each hand start from arms back position. Punch alternate arms vertically.

(9) *Skipping.* Vary the skipping steps and work as fast as possible.

(10) *Interval Running.* Jog along slowly for 50 yds, then sprint for 20 yds.

HOW TO USE THESE EXERCISES

(A) *Circuit Training*

(1) Select nine or ten exercises from the list—do not include Interval Running which should be done after completing circuit training and, if possible, on non-circuit days.

(2) At the first session perform each exercise in turn for 30 seconds (or until you can do no more) and record the number of repetitions done. This is your TEST RATE. It is important to go through the full range of movement at each exercise. To get your TRAINING RATE at each exercise, halve the TEST RATE.

(3) At the second session perform each exercise at the TRAINING RATE. Then repeat so that you have performed each exercise twice. Time yourself from the start of the first exercise to the end of the last one. Record time taken. After a short rest commence Interval Running for 5–10 minutes.

(4) Third, fourth, fifth and sixth session as for second session.

(5) Seventh and all subsequent sessions—Do the circuit three times instead of two at same Training Rate.

(6) Record the total time taken for each session. After several weeks you should notice that the time has been reduced. When the margin by which it is reduced each session becomes only a few seconds or when you cannot reduce it at all it is time to re-test your capacity as in (2) above. You should find that your

Appendix A

TEST RATE has risen as a result of the work you have done. This is positive proof that you are now fitter.

(7) Use a chart like the one below to record your progress.

No.	EXERCISE	Date Test	TRNG RATE	Date Test	TRNG RATE	Date Test	TRNG RATE
1							
2							
3							
4							
5							
6							
7							
8							
9							
10							

DATE	TIME TAKEN	DATE	TIME TAKEN	DATE	TIME TAKEN	DATE	TIME TAKEN	DATE	TIME TAKEN

(B) *General*

(1) Train as above at least twice a week but preferably three times. (However, if you are doing similar work regularly in the gym at school, then you will not need to do this programme as often. The best person to advise you about this is your Physical

165

Appendix A

Education Master at school or whoever is supervising your training.)

(2) Always get thoroughly warm before starting circuit training by spending a few minutes jogging round a track (or road) and doing a few limbering up exercises. It is important to get the blood flowing in the muscles which you are about to exercise.

(3) Do not be surprised if the first two or three sessions leave you feeling stiff the following day. In fact if you do not feel stiff you are probably not doing the exercises properly. A few minutes spent limbering up will soon remove the stiffness.

(4) Training done as suggested above in competition with your own past performance and the clock can be enjoyable. But remember that training is not an end in itself; its purpose is to make you better equipped, both physically and mentally, to play better tennis.